PITTSBURGH THEOLOGICAL MONOGRAPH SERIES

General Editor
Dikran Y. Hadidian

24

The Bursting of New Wineskins
Reflections on religion and culture
at the end of affluence

The Bursting Of New Wineskins

Reflections On Religion and Culture At The End Of Affluence

by
CARL A. RASCHKE

PICKWICK PUBLICATIONS
An imprint of *Wipf and Stock Publishers*
199 West 8th Avenue • Eugene OR 97401

Library of Congress Cataloging in Publication Data

Raschke, Carl A.
  The bursting of new wineskins.

  (Pittsburgh theological monograph series ; 24)
  1. Sociology, Christian. 2. Wealth--Moral and
religious aspects. 3. Liberalism (Religion)--United
States. I. Title. II. Series.
BT738.R32   261.8   78-16604
ISBN 0-915138-34-4

                Pickwick Publications
                An imprint of Wipf & Stock Publishers
                199 West 8th Avenue, Suite 3
                Eugene, Oregon 97401

                The Bursting of New Wineskins
                Reflections on Religion and Culture at the End of Affluence
                By Raschke, Carl A.
                Copyright©1978 by Raschke, Carl A.
                ISBN: 0-915138-34-4
                Publication date 1/1/1978

CONTENTS

PREFACE vii

Chapter

1. THE END OF AFFLUENCE 1

   The Conventional Wisdom
   The Revolution of Falling Expectations
   The Paradox of Productivity
   The Energy Joker in the Deck
   The Switch to Permanence

2. THE BURSTING OF NEW WINESKINS: THE OBSOLESCENCE
   OF POPULAR LIBERAL THEOLOGY 21

   The Passion for Innovation
   The Habit of Privatism
   The Seduction of Affluence
   The Limits of Action

3. THE DARK NIGHT OF THE PERSON. 53

   The Landscape of Homelessness
   The Dark Night of the Person
   Psychorelioiosity: The Opium of the Middle Classes
   Theology and the Search for a Center

4. THE RECOVERY OF TRADITION 85

   Tradition and Modernity
   Affluence, Conservatism, and Totalitarianism
   The Need for New Traditions
   The Cores of Tradition: Communes, Co-operatives
   or Neighborhoods?
   The Church

5. THE FAMILY OF GOD 115

   The Affluent Family
   Affluence and the Ethos of Autonomy
   Women's Liberation and the Family
   The Family of God

6. THE PURSUIT OF HAPPINESS   149
    Turning Down the Ecstatic
    The Limits of Self-realization
    Toward the Steady State
    The Allotment of Sparse Wealth and the "New" Morality

7. THE TRANSFIGURATION OF TRADITION: A RELIGION
    OF THE OBVIOUS, SIMPLE, APPROPRIATE, AND NATURAL   177
    Trust is the Obvious
    Tradition and Simplicity
    On Doing What is Appropriate
    Naturalism and Personalism
    Man and Woman: The Form of the Natural

A THEOLOGICAL POSTSCRIPT   211
    The End of History
    The Second Coming
    Beyond Idolatry
    The Living God
    Summation

PREFACE

The recurring economic crises, or near crises, of the past five years have slowly impressed the public mind that we have moved into an era signaling the "end of affluence." The source as well as the visible symptom of these crises has been the increasing shortages of energy, which have made the average American realize that his habitual, wasteful life-style of uninhibited consumption is rapidly becoming impractical. At the same time, much has been written about the economic factors and problems associated with dwindling energy supplies, and there has been a good deal of offhanded speculation about imminent changes in social arrangements that must accompany the slowdown in economic growth. Yet theological reflection concerning the impact of diminished wealth on religious attitudes and values, and the social expectations underlying them, has been minimal; or at least it has not been done in a sustained and comprehensive way.

In the following pages the author assumes the task of such sweeping reflection. The book begins in the first chapter with a hard look at the "conventional wisdom" about economic growth which has permeated contemporary American social thinking and which is still difficult to shake off, even in the face of radically altered historical circumstances. Chapter two applies this kind of analysis to the sociological assumptions that have undergirded theological writing since the 1960s, particularly the varied strand of thinking taken generally as Protestant "liberalism." The author argues that the "radical" movements of theology in the 1960s and early 1970s were not radical at all, but a sort of disguised, self-indulgent celebration of the values and sensitivities of the affluent middle-classes. The end of affluence, therefore, severely undercuts the hidden presuppositions of these movements. The third chapter examines and carries through this exposition with a special focus on the cult of personal "growth" and "self-actualization" manifest in the "Human Potential Movement." The author maintains that the concept of the "person," so fundamental to the "growth" ideal, is a pernicious abstraction that reflects a breakdown of significant historical and communal links between human beings for which affluence is responsible. Chapter four addresses itself to the question of how the social order can be remade (indeed, how such a remaking is imperative) in light of the new economic reality. The key to such a reintegration of society is a recovery of the sense of "tradition." Chapters five and six refine this notion by concentration on the problem of the disintegrating family and by a thorough reconsideration of the time-honored principle of the "pursuit of happiness." Chapter seven launches into some guarded futurological speculations about what shape a post affluent society with a new feeling for "tradition" might take, and about what might be the new religious orientations and moral values implicit in such a social structure. Finally, the postscript broaches the specific tasks Christian theology as an autonomous discipline must confront.

The publication of this book has been a long and arduous task since completion of the first draft of the manuscript in early 1976. Because of the swift pace of current social history, some of the references or illustrations may seem slightly dated, yet the fundamental drift of thought and culture over the last few years has not changed to such an extent that the author might wish to revise his position. In fact, recent events seem to corroborate the position even more firmly.

The author wishes to extend the following acknowledgements of appreciation to persons who have aided in the preparation of the manuscript and publication of the book:

> Gretchen Hawley and Sandra Sullivan for assistance in typing; Tracy Surber for typing and research; Dr. Walter R. Clyde of Pittsburgh Theological Seminary for extensive editorial review; and finally to the University of Denver for a faculty research grant to fund various aspects of publication.

Carl A. Raschke

Denver, Colorado
December 1977

CHAPTER 1

The End of Affluence

> "In some measure the articulation of the
> conventional wisdom is a religious rite. It is
> an act of affirmation like reading aloud from
> the Scriptures or going to church."
>
> -- John Kenneth Galbraith,
> *The Affluent Society*

The Conventional Wisdom

Like the "sacred doctrine" of church theologians, the "conventional wisdom" of economists has seldom varied much. Derided by Galbraith almost two decades ago, it was the unexamined belief that an ever increasing output of goods and services in the economy constitutes the highest good which government policy-makers should seek to realize. Indeed, it was Galbraith's book which gave the term "affluence" itself wide circulation. "Affluence," as the etymology of the word indicates, means a process of "flowing to" or "flowing abundantly;" and the flood of goods in the mid-twentieth century American economy, far overspreading the margins of necessity, moved Galbraith to question whether sufficiency had become excess, whether the hypertrophy of national wealth and the assumed conquest of poverty had led overnight into an obsession with production and consumption for its own sake.

Galbraith was himself puzzled because the steady elimination of want had engendered even greater want, and the reduction of scarcity by the most formidable economic machinery the world had ever known did *not* result in more satisfaction with life on the part of consumers. Galbraith described the irony as follows: "Why is it that as production has increased in modern times concern for production seems also to have increased?"[1] In other words, the more the modern American economy proved itself capable of spewing out refrigerators, automobiles, and television sets, over and above staples like food and clothing, the faster it kept gearing itself to turn out even larger masses of these items. It depended even more on the insatiable appetites of ordinary buyers who were expected to demand without pause ever improved and diverse goods.

Galbraith sized up the "problem" of affluence as that of a society which manufactured too much of what it really needed. The American economy unflaggingly provided goodies until its clients were fat and bloated. Galbraith envisioned the need to divert resources for the advancement of private material gain into public works, such as schools and medical services, or into cultural and artistic enterprises. The social revolt arose out of much the same sort of uneasiness with the morality of affluence. The vast, visible wealth of the mightiest nation on earth was composed chiefly of crass and cloying possessions or pastimes like Chevrolets with outsize fenders or electric garage door openers, power lawn mowers or decorative gas lamps. The Vietnam War, which stimulated defense contractors to turn out lethal military munitions and material, only heightened awareness of how warped the method of allocating the country's social product had become, how empty the term "productivity" seemed. Thus, social critics of the period clamored for a resetting of "priorities," a downgrading of useless production in order to meet more communal, esthetic, or "spiritual" needs.

The conventional wisdom remained, however, as to what was best for the economy. Productivity was still viewed by both professional economists and the homebodies as significant only with respect to quantity, not quality. Napalm and self-erasing typewriters counted as much in the computation of the Gross

National Product (GNP) as good books or a new pair of bifocals. President Nixon's Labor Day address to the nation in 1971 was the last grand testimony to the ancient faith. The fact that he saw the encouragement of new car sales as perhaps the top item on the national business agenda only underlined the tenacity of the conventional wisdom. But then in 1973 a funny thing happened. Inflation began to soar. Both food and new cars became incredibly expensive, and the decline in the average worker's purchasing power seemed unstoppable. The problem of "affluence" seemed to be solving itself, remorselessly, by a slow collapse of the affluent economy itself.

In the last several years there has been a growing awareness, not just among prophets of doom but throughout the populace itself, that we have arrived at the end of affluence. The drift from recession to inflation, and "back" to recession and inflation together, has left a feeling abroad in the land that there are fundamental structural deficiencies in our economy. Moreover, awareness of these deficiencies, combined with the mirage of true economic "recovery," has precipitated hard examination of the key premises of affluence. It is being examined not just as an issue of life-style or taste. For example, is it injurious to the soul for everyone to have his own suburban ranch home with potted chrysanthemums? Affluence is being examined as a basic threat to survival. Has our present economic system, in the end, failed to deliver even the basic goods and services?

The conventional wisdom was still intoned by the Ford Administration throughout 1975 and 1976 to the effect that affluence or "prosperity," as we have recently known it, could and should be recaptured. The strategy of increasing output continued to be invoked with the regularity of a priest reciting the *pater noster*. However, the faithful showed themselves less likely to go on participating in the solemn rites. Opinion samplings, including those of Gallup, have indicated that

Americans have little "confidence" left in politicians who promise "more of the same." There are also indications that the public is acclimatizing itself faster than its elected spokesmen to the forecast of lowered living standards and may in truth be on the verge of accepting a whole new *ethos* of frugality and simplicity. Predictions of wholesale shifts in public sentiments, however, are precarious at best, and it is not the task of this book to harp on them. What counts is that the conventional wisdom of recent decades, if not that of the post-Civil War period, has shattered against sharp, new economic realities. These realities are unmistakable; and it thus becomes the job of professionals and lay people alike to evaluate what larger changes in our habits of thinking and desiring *ought* to come about in response to such realities.

The Revolution of Falling Expectations

It used to be a truism among sociologists and political scientists that we were living through an era of "rising expectations." The revolutionary militancy of minority groups and the push for higher wages by unions in this country were regarded, along with the drive for development throughout the Third World, as expressions of a broader clamor among the disadvantaged for a stake in the new prosperity. The phenomenon of rising expectations could be explained from the reaction of those who historically had been have-nots. They were viewing the tremendous progress and economic success among the haves with both hope and envy. Since so much wealth was now available, it was only right that they be entitled to share it.

By and large the haves at least paid lip service to these aspirations. The ballyhooed foreign development programs under the Kennedy Administration, as exemplified in the Peace Corps and Alliance for Progress, were affluent America's gesture to its indigent international competitors. The Great Society legislation during the Johnson Years -- the expansion of welfare, educational, cultural, and political opportunities for the deprived in our midst -- was conceived and executed in the spirit of parceling out abundance. The typical liberal complaint was that something must be amiss with a society which produces so much, yet leaves some of its citizens to fend for themselves and skimp by. The drafting of social programs to allay want and inequality raised the morale of many who had formerly felt the desperation of life-long need, and gradually inspired them to count on even more.

Unfortunately, the spoils of affluence still tended to go to the haves more than to the have-nots. Social services bureaucrats were hired with fat salaries; regular government workers padded their earnings benefiting themselves much more than the unfortunates they were supposed to be serving. The 1960's, it seems in retrospect, did lift the lot of many who were formerly at the bottom of the social status hierarchy. Yet the gap between rich and poor as a whole did not narrow much, and in many instances actually widened. Thus the invitation was open to pragmatic policy advocates such as Peter Passell and Leonard Ross to argue that the solution to the inequities of affluence was more affluence for everybody. The poor could never depend on the rich to make real sacrifices in their behalf, but they could expect their more advantaged brethren, as trustees of burgeoning wealth, to make more available for everybody.[2] Such a position amounted to a general social version of the "trickle down" or "tossed crumbs" theory of wealth and consumption -- the idea that those who want get what those who want not have left over. And it is fair to say that the theory was applied for many years quite unconsciously through government programs.

But the promise of continually multiplying wealth was contradicted by the major economic crisis that emerged full-bloom in 1973 with runaway inflation, the international monetary crisis, and then the Arab oil embargo. The deep recession, accentuated by the leap in unemployment at the close of 1974, shattered the comfortable ideology of the previous generation, and produced what some recent commentators have wryly dubbed "the revolution of falling expectations." The amiable assumption that the riveter in Detroit, or the shipping clerk in San Francisco, could rest confident that in future years he would probably make more and work less, was countermanded by the grim knowledge that exactly the opposite seemed likely. Even if through collective bargaining he could win successive salary raises, the odds were that inflation would eat up his increased pay check, or he would be laid off and his gains would not matter anyway, or the company would go out of business and his wage contract made void.

As for more government spending, that meant for him not benefits, but higher taxes or inflation. Losing trust in government he was willing to permit Congress, or his state, or his local government to lop off services that in the past, out of conscience, he could have demanded. In 1974 California elected as its governor a "liberal" Democrat who within less than a year was more parsimonious than his Republican predecessor, and who won the support of 86 percent of the people, according to one poll, because he preached a gospel of letting the state do less for its citizens. As George Will wrote in *Newsweek* of Jerry Brown's political philosophy: "What ruins individuals and nations is overdeveloped appetites, which are stimulated by the illusion that mankind has escaped the constraints of scarcity. The government has nourished this illusion. It has tried to be all things to all people, or at least as many things to as many people as possible in order to spur consumption generally..."[3] Not only did the worker expect his private situation *not* to improve; he also disavowed the ability of his elected representatives to do much about it.

His only concern, probably, was that in a period of scarcity others did not suffer as much as he did.

The mood of falling expectations most likely accounted for the mysterious fact that unemployment of 9.2% in early 1975 did not lead immediately to rioting in the streets or to activity no more revolutionary than the election of a heavily Democratic congress in the fall of 1974. Rising expectations, it has been said, beget revolution; falling expectations eventuate in resignation, cynicism, or withdrawal. Falling expectations have not raised a hue and cry for the return of affluence so much as they have brought about disenchantment with affluence and openness to a critique of it.

The Paradox of Productivity

The crisis of affluence, it may be argued without straining the point too much, is really owing to the temporary "successes" of the Western industrial system since the Second World War. Such "successes" are exhibited by the fantastic rise in raw output of the system as measured in the impressive and beguiling annual GNP figures. The conventional economic wisdom has applauded these successes and incorporated them into its larger theory about the purposes of economic man. Twentieth century economic theory, often referred to as "neo-classical" economics, has refined the nineteenth century model of man as a creature with limitless wants who strives to maximize his "happiness" within the bounds of available productive resources, e.g., land, labor, and capital. It has emphasized output or productivity as evidence of proper economic activity. To this, as a goad to industrial production, so-called Keynsean economics has merely annexed the importance of social demand or "consumption," and introduced state intervention as a strategy for keeping the two factors in balance. Profit, the

key to economic well-being in the classical view, was laid
respectfully alongside the social utility of goods and services.
Thus the capacity of the system to generate employment, incomes,
and buying power leading to the production of more goods and
services, was the test of whether all is right within this best
of material worlds.

So long as the system more than worked to its capacity,
the economic criteria for describing and evaluating it did
not come under any serious scrutiny. When the system began to
falter in the late 1960's, opportunity for questioning presented
itself. In *The Affluent Society* Galbraith challenged wanton
production of superfluous wealth at the expense of social services and the arts. Yet the contradiction between the ease by
which society could buy transistor radios and automobile acces-
sories, and its neglect of basic necessities, became fully
conspicuous only recently. In his book, *Economics and the
Public Purpose*, Galbraith raged even more prophetically:

> With economic development the contrast between
> the houses in which the masses of people live, the
> medical and hospital services they can afford and
> the conveyances into which they are jammed and the
> other and more frivolous components of their living
> standard -- automobiles, television, cosmetic, in-
> toxicants -- becomes first striking and then obscene.[4]

Galbraith's pronouncement is made about as forceful as can be
by the great inflation beginning in 1973. It was powered by
runaway costs of necessities such as food, fuel, and medical
care (new cars being an interesting exception at the outset)
that have accented the contrasts among the components in the
American living standard, even for middle-class families, to
which Galbraith refers.

The touted productivity of the system has met with disillusionment because in the long run it has given us cheap
luxuries and expensive necessities. In 1973 there were

shortages of beef and toilet paper but a plethora of tennis balls and cologne. In 1975 one usually paid more for a yearly health insurance premium than for an "expensive" set of stereo components. Productivity had been certified as an end in itself so that any discrimination as to what was being produced and who might benefit from it had been abandoned. When William Simon, the Secretary of the Treasury, urged that more petroleum be produced without real concern for who might be able to afford it, the bankruptcy of modern economic reasoning showed its colors. The health of the economy was estimated by administration advisors according to the capacity of businesses, regardless of their mission to society, to produce more and to make more profits, even without sufficient consumption. Democratic economists were often bent upon promoting full employment and maximum consumption, even if it meant higher inflation and renewed shortages. The quality or effects of production and consumption were ignored for the sake of quantity, that is, aggregate output and aggregate utilization of goods and services. One did not consider whether there might be any genuine value or purpose in producing new cars. Republicans wanted Detroit to become more attractive to its stockholders; Democrats wanted the auto workers to go back to work.

  In short, affluence in the modern world has come, in the minds of many, to be self-justifying. It has come to be legitimated not so much through whom or how it benefits, or through what higher moral or social ends it serves, but through its own perpetuation. Self-justifying behavior has often been imputed to corporations, politicians, and government bureaucrats, but seldom to the economic system as a whole. The irony of such a situation, or what we shall call the "paradox of productivity," rests on the special conditions by which affluence has emerged and by which it has sustained itself. The failure to grasp the inherent self-destructiveness of an affluent economy can only retard sensible economic reform. The mystifying unresponsiveness of the system to present economic policy is not so mystifying when understood in light of the very nature of affluence and the disappearance of the special conditions ensuring it.

The paradox of productivity is in part the product of the success of the affluent society. As the old saw has it: success breeds it own failures. The paradox of productivity is also in part the product of the complexity of the affluent society. The rule is that the more complex a system is the more vulnerable a system is at a greater magnitude, the more potential it has for disruption. A flimsily built car hurtling along the highway at high speed runs a greater risk of crashing and killing its occupants than if it were sturdy, or if it were moving more slowly. The "drivers" of the present system have now lost control of their vehicle and are careening toward disaster. In truth, it is the "speed" of the vehicle more than its structure that is causing the problem.

We must remember that "affluence" implies flow or "speed." An affluent economy is not gauged so much by "what" citizens possess in the qualitative sense, but by "how" much they possess and how easy it is for them to divest themselves of their possessions and acquire new ones. In other words, an affluent society is affluent because many goods are produced and services are performed. Furthermore, it is affluent not so much because many goods and services "flow" through the economy, but because they flow at a rapid rate. Introductory economic textbooks tell us that the "amount" of money in a modern economy is a function of the speed at which money is passed from one hand to the next. Money is nothing if it is not spent, and up to a point it becomes more valuable if transmitted rapidly from consumer to producer and back to the consumer again.[6]

investment must temporarily come from decreased consumption in the economy as a whole, through lower wages for workers or through higher prices. In the post-war economy lower wages for workers were ruled out by the bargaining-power of organized labor; significantly higher prices would tend to cut consumption and hence decrease income for new investment. Thus the inevitable tendency was to undertake capital formation by way of new technologies. New technologies, though, are made expensive by the costs of research and the competitive price of specially trained personnel.

The solution to the costs of research and development was to further capital expansion by the application of energy intensive technology. The problem of high labor costs was met by heavier infusions of cheap energy into the productive apparatus. Early capital expansion in the United States was accomplished by the employment of cheap labor. Later capitalist expansion was brought about through reliance on inexpensive natural resources, particularly energy. For a while the abundance of foreign energy resources counterbalanced the threat of dwindling domestic stocks. Then, finally the end of cheap energy resources eroded the base upon which rising productivity was made possible.

Kenneth Boulding has noted that "economic growth is closely associated with rising energy inputs from fossil fuels."[8] The over-utilization or "waste" of fossil fuels as a condition of rising productivity has merely hastened the day when the energy "fix" behind continuing growth can no longer sustain the desired effects. The dissipation of known energy deposits cannot be offset by new forms of retrieval in increasingly exotic places. The reason is simple. The cost of extraction of such deposits rises proportionately with the remoteness of their location and the difficulty in obtaining them. New technologies for mining or drilling come with an expensive invoice.[9]

Dennis Meadows, author of *The Limits to Growth*, has remarked that "given present resource consumption rates and the projected increase in these rates, the great majority of the currently important nonrenewable resources will be extremely costly 100 years from now."[10] But steady economic growth depends on the retention of cheap energy sources. With the shrinking of such sources, according to Meadows, economic growth reaches its natural limits. To go all out to provide more energy through extensive exploration and technical innovation upsets the rationale of an energy intensive economy, the providing of less costly substitutes for human labor, and curbs growth. Easy availability and abundant petroleum made it important in the developing of general affluence. Without it the promise of preserving affluence grows strikingly hollow.

Thus, the end of affluence has been precipitated by shortages of the very energy which formerly served to accelerate productivity and boost the general standard of living. Just as an electric water pump will cease circulating fluid at a rapid rate through a network of pipes when its current has been shut off, so the flow of goods and services in the affluent economy must taper off as energy inputs are blocked. Neither neo-classical nor Keynsian economics understood or cared about the energy variable in calculating the performance of an economic system. Energy was theoretically inexhaustible and thus economically irrelevant as a factor in production. The problem of growth was simple. Get people to spend more and industry will churn out more things for them to consume. Production and consumption, however, have a more restricted significance when their pace is bound with the prospect of scouring out the earth's bounty. The character and amount of what is produced or consumed become more at issue than the bare quantity of output.

The weakness of an energy intensive economy thus is exposed. With cheap energy gone our ingrained social habits of waste and

and systematic consumption prove more harmful than beneficial to a "decent" standard of living. What is gimcrack and shabby can no longer be accepted as a "good buy;" when it falls apart, we may experience difficulty purchasing a new one. Those who confront the stiff costs of new automobiles today are probably more impressed with quality than in times past. With the end of affluence the conventional standard of wealth will have to shift from how briskly we consume to how long we can preserve what we have. We will ask ourselves which is better -- to buy a new pair of blue jeans every six months, or to own a good one that lasts for two years.

The Switch to Permanence

Conserving will probably become, therefore, the password to the culture bound to develop with the end of affluence. In recent years we have witnessed a resurgence of the conservation ethic principally among the ecology set. Conservation here was largely a matter of esthetics, or derived from some kind of intuitive veneration for Douglas firs and harbor seals and the fear of endangered health from pollutants and toxic chemicals in our food or water. Conservation, however, must necessarily become an essential of survival. We will have to learn to do with what we have, and to make the most of what we have. Such a switch in attitudes about what should be expected, accepted, and prized in our everyday comings and goings will affect not just our material exchanges but also our very values, symbols, beliefs, and other particulars of culture. We will have to move from a culture that has institutionalized rapid change and turnover to one that banks on continuity and stability. We will have to give up our current rapture with everything "new" -- not just new motorcycles, new boats, and new brassieres, but also new moralities and new intellectual furors

that foam up like bubbles and burst in seconds. We will have
to learn to conserve what is truly best in life and abide with
it for its own worth. Such a change may be the most painful
and awkward that we have had to face in this much bruited "age
of change." To hang on to and relish the permanent or enduring
may prove a *tour de force* for a culture which has hypnotized
itself with the spurious expectation of constant change and
growth.

In the last analysis the end of affluence, or of the limits
of growth, is perhaps more a religious and moral challenge than
a strictly economic one. The challenge is one of building a
religious vision of man in the universe that takes into account
his place in society and comes to terms with the stark reality
of scarcity. It is one of finding an alternative posture to a
facile faith in growth. Tom O'Brien has noted that "growth"
has recurrently

> functioned like a secular religion...(It) has
> served as a rationale for the propertied classes
> which they use to forestall toward an indefinite
> future the satisfaction of needs; like the old
> time religion, moreover, for the masses of man-
> kind at least, growth increasingly threatens never
> to deliver the goods, and to keep its pie in the
> sky, permanently frozen.[11]

The end of affluence will very likely induce a general reassessment of growth itself and a tough look at how it has
created social imbalances and injustices, how it has nurtured
false needs and desires along with bogus symbols and values.
The failure of the affluent society ultimately to "deliver
the goods" helps to call into question the legitimacy of such
a secular religion of growth, and bids reflection on more
natural ways of perceiving the world forms of "worship" richer
than the idolatry of the newer, bigger, and better. The limits
of growth throws into clear view the very limits of our vain
imaginings and social fantasies. It brings into awareness the

hollowness of our rhetoric, especially among those who have somehow come to think that permanence is a scurvy knave and that, in Aeschylus' words, "whirl is king" before whom we ought to prostrate ourselves.

We will go on to explore the manner in which the cult of the obsolete has in itself become obsolete, how the new has become old-fashioned, how growth truly implies stagnation. We will pursue the various subtleties and undertones of the now aging "secular religion" which has infested the thinking of more than one generation. But first we will look at contemporary religion, and how the theology of the secular gospel dominates even the latest claims on behalf of the sacred.

NOTES TO CHAPTER 1

1. John Kenneth Galbraith, *The Affluent Society* (Boston: Houghton Mifflin & Co., 1958), p. 120.

2. See Peter Passels and Leonard Ross, *The Retreat from Riches: Affluence and its Enemies* (New York: Viking Press, 1973).

3. George Will, "Cool Hand Jerry," *Newsweek* (Nov. 10, 1975), p. 3.

4. John Kenneth Galbraith, *Economics and the Public Purpose* (New York: Houghton Mifflin & Co., 1973), pp. 267-8.

5. There are several reasons for this state of affairs. First, since the health industry in the United States has traditionally been run on a profit footing and under the direction of the monopolistic American Medical Association, the usual laws of supply and demand have not functioned for medical services. Second, health care has never been a consumer "option" which can be rejected or deferred by the users of the service, and this has led to greatly inflated cost increases, now double and sometimes triple the average rise in the cost of living. Exotic and expensive equipment for diagnosis and therapy has been freely used by hospitals without the typical incentives for cost containment. Third, the method of indirect payments for services through Medicare, Medicaid, and private health insurance has sometimes encouraged waste of health resources which might not be as pronounced were the patient obliged to pay directly for them himself.

6. See Paul Samuelson, *Economics* (New York: McGraw Hill, 1964), 6th edition, p. 278ff.

7. Keynes' example is obviously an extreme one, but it points up the fundamental difficulty with the definition of "wealth" implicit in all forms of neo-classical economics.

8. This quotation comes from an article syndicated in 1975 by a number of national newspapers.

9. Dr. Eneas Kane, vice-president for Technology of Standard Oil of California, has estimated that the present cost of solar energy for generating electricity and for conversion into other kinds of energy other than that the heating of homes, which is also the major area where alternative fuel development will be vital, works out to about a $4,000 equivalent

for a barrel of crude oil. The current OPEC price for a barrel of crude, in comparison, is $12-$13 per barrel. See an interview with Dr. Kane in "Alternate Fuels," *Bulletin of the Standard Oil Company of California* (Fall 1976), p. 6.

10. D. and D. H. Meadows, *The Limits to Growth* (New York: New American Library, 1973), p. 74.

11. Tom O'Brien, "Marrying Malthus and Marx," *Environmental Action* (August 30, 1975), p. 6.

CHAPTER 2

The Bursting of New Wineskins: The Obsolescence of Popular Liberal Theology

"Whom will he teach knowledge, and to whom will he
   explain the message?
Those who are weaned from the milk, those taken
   from the breast?
For it is precept upon precept, precept upon precept,
   line upon line, line upon line, here a little,
   there a little."

Nay, but by men of strange lips and with an alien
   tongue the Lord will speak to this people, to
   whom he has said, "This is rest; give rest to
   the weary; and this is repose;" yet they would
   not hear.

Therefore the word of the Lord will be to them precept
   upon precept, precept upon precept, line upon
   line, line upon line, here a little, there a
   little; that they may go, and fall backward, and
   be broken, and snared, and taken.

---Isaiah 28:9-13

The Passion for Innovation

Liberal theology, since its genesis in the German Romantic movement of the nineteenth century, has recurrently stressed the need for new models and methods of interpreting Christian faith that bend with the times while challenging the ruling orthodoxies and outworn forms of meaning. For over a century and a half such theology established itself, despite the brief *interregnum* of neo-orthodoxy before and after the Second World War, as the leading negotiator between a Christianity on the defensive and modern, secular culture. In such a role, liberal theology has more often than not taken the side of whatever mode of secular culture happened to predominate, as Karl Barth astutely perceived. Whether as conservative "cultural Protestantism" in nineteenth century Germany, or as part of the more innovative "secular gospel" that stormed America during the early 1960's, liberal Protestantism leaned with the wind and took upon itself the morals and manners of a particular social or intellectual group that would command attention in a given generation.

Parrying the often obscurantist and uninspired objections of its critics, liberal theology served as a plumbline within the churches for measuring the response of faith to changed historical conditions. The ancient Hebrews had shaped their interpretation of revelation around the ongoing activity of God in history, and Christians before Constantine had carried through the process of creative renewal in the understanding of man's historical situation. The early Christians, in contrast with their pagan adversaries, who in the myths and rites of traditional piety clung to the idea of an eternal, cosmic order of life, remained open to the possibility of new religious encounters, or what we might call "God's surprises." Their openness to religious encounter ensured a critical perspective on human morality, social practices, and institutions. Up to a point the same was true of liberal theology. Liberal theology prevented modern Christianity from backsliding into medieval dogmatism and triumphalism. In other words, it kept Christianity *historical*.

The pressure for historical adaptation, however, became acute by the mid-twentieth century. Technological strides and a succession of world crises had left Western humanity reconciled, if only fearfully, to the fact of history. Only the churches, from the vantage point of the guardians of the new culture, seemed immune to the ideology of constant change and progress. In the early 60's, just when the Kennedy Administration was opening the "New Frontier," the Civil Rights movement was launched, and college students swarmed to serve mankind through the Peace Corps, Christian theology suddenly woke up from its post-war slumber and undertook to clean out all remaining anachronisms within its view of man and the world. Harking back to the murky prophecy of a "religionless Christianity" uttered by the martyred German theologian, Dietrich Bonhoeffer, during his imprisonment by the Nazis, some theologians called for a new marriage of theology with the *saeculum*. Harvey Cox's book, *The Secular City*, published in 1964, set the tone for this frontal assault on the prevailing "otherworldliness" of the churches. Then followed in rapid succession the "death of God" movement, "radical theology," "the theology of hope," and the multifaceted "liberation theology," not to mention the sundry flirtations with sex, ecstasy, and mysticism under the general rubric of "the theology of play."

The watchword of popular liberal theology in the 1960's was "newness." "Newness," however, came to connote not so much a gradual reformation of the tradition so much as a frenzied scramble for the unique and the untried which sometimes bordered on the shocking. Not only were time-honored concepts and dispositions overthrown, but each breaking wave of theological novelty had the effect of superseding (we might say "one-upping") what had just gone before. One style of popular liberal theology was first assailed as pedantic, complacent, soporific, or irrelevant; the next for its bourgeois sympathies; the third for its false universalism and lack of ethnic or cultural sensitivity; the fourth for its tacit sexism which tainted all Western theologizing in the past; etc. Soon Macmillan Co., began issuing a series of volumes entitled "New Theology No. 1," "New Theology No. 2," and so on. Liberal theology became popular and trendy like the pace-setters in mass culture.

The only trouble was that none of these "dramatic" breakthroughs made by popular liberal theology ever left a lasting impact. As with the tempo of fads and counterfads that swirled through the sensation-hungry national media, they came and went like LSD and paisley shirt, and after a few years with only some dated book titles on the publishers' overstock lists left to show. In spite of all the "hoopla" that greeted each new definition of what theology should be if it would keep up with the Cones and the Moltmanns, clergy and academics alike lamented that the field was devoid of the old "giants" such as Tillich, Barth, and Bultmann. It came to a pretty pass when *Christianity & Crisis*, not too long ago, published an issue with commentary by a select handful of religious thinkers who addressed themselves to the disconsolate question, "Whatever happened to theology?"[1]

Theology, it seemed, had died along with the death of God as well as the Beatles and "radical chic." The momentum of forever capturing the new and definitively dazzling had been spent. Popular liberal theology today has gone the way of the 60's. But, like the 60's itself, for which Alvin Toffler's *Future Shock*, in its paean to upbeat culture, rapid change, obsolescence, and transience, was a final tribute, popular liberal theology finds nowadays that it has so overdone the new that it has sundered its own roots and thereby withered from lack of nourishment. Popular liberal theology's case in the 70's is somewhat similar to that of the middle age businessman who in imitation of the new generation belatedly got turned on to Esalen sensitivity weekends, "dropping out," and kinky sex, only to discover shortly thereafter that the kids have now grown conformist, careerminded, and nostalgic for the life he daringly abandoned, and that now he can't go back to the executive suite because no one will have him.

For all its gimmickry and temporizing, though, popular liberal theology preserved for a season the receptiveness of Christianity to the historical character of human experience. The Biblical proof text for liberal theology's method could well be the incident in the Synoptic Gospels involving Jesus and the Pharisees. The Pharisees reprove Jesus' disciples for not observing the convention of fasting. The Pharisees find fault with Jesus for relying too much on his own intuitions of the truth without proper deference to long-standing tradition. Jesus answers, characteristically, in the language of metaphor and parable.

> No one sews a piece of unshrunk cloth on an old garment; if he does, the patch tears away from it, the new from the old, and a worse tear is made. And no one puts new wine into old wineskins; if he does, the wine will burst the skins, and the wine is lost, and so are the skins; but new wine is for fresh skins. (Mark 2:21-22)

The "new wine" of present experience is no longer adequate for the old cultural and symbolic containers. Should the guardians of tradition seek to squeeze the prophet's message into aged forms of meaning, they will destroy both the old concepts and the new inspiration.

The revelatory tone of the more *avant-garde* theologies in the 1960's tended to suggest to many that old-style Christian hermeneutic could no longer suffice for the distinctly contemporary gospel that grew out of the turbulent times. Thus

many heralds of the new message found by and by not only the
wisdom of the immediate forefathers, but the entire Christian
legacy wanting. Other religions of the world, especially those
with a non-Western or non-theistic flavor, seemed more congenial
to their task. Those who could not handle or resonate with the
esoteric schools of the East opted for the "heretical" philosophies or cults which had once seemed inimical to normative
Christianity, such as pagan vitalism or the ideas of Nietzsche.
Sam Keen coined the term "new Dionysianism,"[2] and David Miller
the term "a new paganism."[3]

The new "wine" grew so heady, however, that it left a
painful hangover. At last it became so pungent that it burst
the new wineskins. The excesses of popular liberal theology,
serving though they did to shake free the spirit of contemporary
man from the shackles of archaic thought patterns, did not
lead to the building of a viable new kind of faith or culture
that would guarantee a solid foundation for the future. Popular
liberal theology left in its wake only a wreckage of former
symbols and values, then stalked quietly away.

The present crisis of popular liberal theology, however,
has not been due solely to its uncritical experimentalism, nor
to its iconoclasm and in some cases its nihilism, though such
corrosives on an established religious community have been
telling. The crisis derives also from the fact that, despite
all its pretensions to innovation, the liberal theology of the
past decade was not innovative enough. The deception of liberal
theology, in many respects, reflected the self-deception of so
many intellectuals and other members of the cultural elite
throughout the 60's. The *avant-garde* theories of the 60's
turned out, in retrospect, to have been less searching and
untinged with privilege and self-interest than its advocates
would ever have concede. The fashionable thing was to excoriate
all aspects of middle-class living, though the new standards of

value which the various movements urged required, if only implicitly, the maintenance of society to a large extent in its customary form. The real change in society, which has come about by impersonal economic forces that no posturing about the evils of American technology or the "one-dimensional" quality of daily existence could ever have precipitated, has required a reassessment of the principles on which effective cultural criticism is based. Liberal theology in particular will be forced in the future, if it has not been already, to turn its vendetta against conventional social norms and attitudes into a will to self-criticism. The speck in the eye of conventional society has been matched by the log in the pupils of many liberal theologians.

The Habit of Privatism

Western society, especially in the American case, has suffered from its emphasis on competitive individualism and on what has come to be called "privatism" in morality and in religious piety. This trait of Western society has hampered the development of an authentic social ethics. Privatism means that the success, comforts, and happiness of the individual take precedence over the common good; what a person does with his own life, even if it affects others directly or indirectly, is no one's business but his own. By the same token, the responsibility for material and spiritual survival rests wholly and squarely on the individual himself. "Bootstrap" salvation in religion (the called-for moral self-perfection which has figured heavily in the preaching of both mainline and sectarian Protestantism for generations) parallels the Horatio Alger mythology for getting ahead in the world of work. Society takes the shape of a loose aggregate of social atoms, traditionless individuals vying with each other in quest of maximum gain and self-enrichment.

"Privatism," therefore, means that a person's private life, which may encompass at its outer limits his family or his ethnic or interest group, counts as the ultimate end toward which he must steer his ambitions or in terms of which he must make all meaningful decisions. Western society has abolished the more traditional idea of binding social duties, except as the discharge of certain obligations in order to enhance one's career or make one respectable in the sight of one's peers. Even the notion of man's duty to God has taken an undetected twist. "God helps those who help themselves" can be translated as, "Everybody ought to help themselves to whatever thay can get, and God will wink approvingly."

An older expression of privatism in religion has been the "New Thought" movement, distilled in the elementary philosophy of life that Norman Vincent Peale several decades ago labelled in his book by the same title, "the power of positive thinking." Peale's pitch, which delighted millions of readers, conveniently decorated the native American drive for success with some slim, liberal Christian apologetics. The opening lines of *The Power of Positive Thinking* betray this strategy. "Believe in yourself! Have faith in your abilities."[4] Throughout his countless sermons, television appearances, magazine articles, and best-selling books, Peale drummed on the theme of personal power and achievement through the "right" frame of mind, which presumably had something remotely to do with being a Christian. The Biblical and prophetic concern with sin and corporate responsibility, however, was understandably missing. A typical use of Biblical "theology" in *The Power of Positive Thinking* was Peale's example of a major league pitcher who found he could win games when he recited a passage from Isaiah over and over again to himself.

Donald Meyer, in his brilliant historical study entitled *The Positive Thinkers*, has traced how "popular psychologies" masquerading as religion, mainly Christianity, have promised

power, wealth, and self-mastery for over a century, beginning
perhaps as far back as Mary Baker Eddy.[5] Meyer notes how
positive thinking, or what he dubs in general "mind cure," has
served millions of men and women caught in the toils of self-
doubt because of their inability to succeed in a competitive
system, giving them the "confidence of God" to be outstanding
business people or civic leaders. The only drawback has been
that mind cure exclusively identified the faith with "faith in
oneself," love with "self-love," and redemption with "self-
improvement." Mind cure, or positive thinking, has proven a
handy rationale for ignoring the dilemmas of interpersonal
involvements or social accountability. Its privatism has been
self-congratulatory and obsessive. An interesting historical
footnote is that just about all of Richard Nixon's inner circle,
before and throughout Watergate, were attracted less by fundamentalist Christianity and more by various mind-cure religions.
Nixon himself regularly went to hear Peale's sermons.

Privatism unfortunately has been the secret stepchild of
popular liberal theology. From Friedrich Schleiermacher, who
early in the last century attempted to assimilate religion to
personal artistic and cultural taste, to William Hamilton, the
erstwhile death-of-God spokesman of the last decade, who defined
"the style of the Christian life" as something akin to "a defense both for ourselves and for the others of the rights of
privacy and solitude,"[6] popular liberal theology has been
consistent. It has eschewed the Biblical stress on divine
power and transcendence in favor of the values of actualizing
one's human potential, worshipping God if it happens to be
conducive to one's creative enrichment, or to just downright
enjoying oneself. To be sure, the latest crop of liberal
theologians have had little truck with the positive thinkers
and the success evangelists. It is not because they do not
covertly share their assumptions about the delights of private

living, but because they view Peale and his ilk as too slickly commercial and crude-middle-class. A good portion of the liberal theologians of the 60's fancied themselves as something other than that. For them to be middle-class was determined not so much by the size of one's salary as by one's insensitivity to each new cultural vogue that came along.

In the 60's the cutting edge between "approved" liberal thinking and "cheap" or "reactionary" theologizing consisted in whether one threw in his lot with the "counterculture." Hardly anyone questioned whether the counterculture was really revolutionary or not. After all, was it not the counterculture which gave the word "revolution" a popular lilt that even Madison Avenue and Richard Nixon picked up or "co-opted," as the counterculture itself would have disdainfully put it. Was it not the counterculture which disinfected the word "revolution" of the older, ideological overtones which had once conjured up in the minds of most Americans the spectre of Moscow-trained cadres besieging Washington? Everything in the 60's from slinging molotov cocktails to wearing miniskirts came to be branded "revolutionary." The result was nothing less than to neutralize the term, to render it just another innocuous and florid catch phrase in pop culture like "right on" or "Pepsi generation."

"Revolution" came to mean not so much a serious and total transformation of the existing order as a spontaneous, unplanned, and somewhat ephemeral event. No wonder, then, that the Woodstock episode, that three-day, mud-soaked revel which came and went like a summer thundershower, struck in the mythology of the counterculture as an image of what the "revolution" was supposed to be. In fine, the "revolutionary" activity of the counterculture amounted to little more than a kind of showmanship and sensationalism which, despite its tendency to make more conservative citizens feel uncomfortable, really did not tamper with the fabric of American life. It was precisely because the revolution was not ultimately threatening, particularly to liberals who stood little chance to lose anything from joining it, that it could be espoused so glibly and with such fanfare.

The revolution of the 60's, and the counterculture which fomented it, when all the shouting was over signaled little more than a renewed pledge to the old American habit of privatism. "Do your own thing," the master slogan of the counterculture which suggested just about all and everything, could readily be taken as a motto for those with the resources to live a self-indulgent and autonomous life-style. In the political sphere, too, it was fairly evident that the "revolution" would incline more toward anarchism than long-range political strategies. Historically, anarchists have not necessarily been those interested in wrestling with the hard problems of eventually creating order in society, or producing enough food to feed the multitudes, of allocating scarce goods and services equitable among the population. Rather, they have been obsessed with the dismantling of all order and authority.

In a democratic or relatively affluent society like the United States or Western Europe, it is very common for privileged individuals or groups to become bored with the traditional leadership roles thrust upon them, and to turn to bohemian life-styles or eccentric brands of politics. The children of the well-to-do professional and administrative classes followed that route in the 60's. And liberal theology, which drew on the sentiments and aspirations of the established clergy and the academic elite in the universities and seminaries, trundled after them. At the risk of oversimplification, we might say that the pseudo-revolutionary rhetoric of so much popular liberal theology relieved many representatives of the privileged groups from having to acknowledge any longer their own privilege. A classic metaphor for the entire era was Leonard Bernstein's famous fund-raising party for the Black Panther Party, where the "beautiful people" of the Eastern social circuit outnumbered ghetto blacks in laughable proportions. Similar things happened when spokesmen for *bona fide* oppressed elements were regaled at Yale or on seminary campuses, and when the United Presbyterian Church decided to contribute funds for the defense of Angela Davis.

These tokens were, of course, newsworthy, but one could hardly conceive of them as parts of a serious revolutionary program. The 60's engendered insurrection against cultural symbols by means of symbols. The "revolutionary theatre" performed by traveling mime troupes in the major cities epitomized the "revolution itself." In this respect it was by and large only a surface disturbance within the collective psyche of the cultural leaders of the affluent middle classes, who really had no reason to jar the system at its foundations. The attacks on such cultural symbols as work, family, country, and sexual fidelity were achieved by means of counter-symbols. In essence the core of American life was left intact. The American habit of privatism bred by affluence over many years has eroded traditional community supports and institutions. The failure of the counterculture to leave an enduring legacy of alternative institutions, and the easy appropriation of many of its values by those in power for their own ends (the sexual revolution of the hippies begat suburban swingers; Oriental mysticism became transcendental meditation for business executives), testify to the preservation of the old ways even amidst the outward appearance of change.

The Seduction of Affluence

The element of privatism in popular liberal theology, moreover, has sprung less from its conceptual quarrel with orthodoxy than with its dependence on conditions of material abundance. In spite of its disaffection with a "soulless" materialism, popular liberal theology has all along assumed

that the "good life" included having all the amenities which
the many mindless robots who work forty hours a week for a
livelihood have come to enjoy. The difference between the
ethics of the counterculture, including by extension that of
popular theology, and the mores of middle America was significant.
While middle-class Americans very readily elevated work
to a kind of sacrament in celebration of the hard-won fruits
of their labor, the counterculture more often than not took
work for granted and even despised it as cramping a higher
"spirituality." "Revolution" presupposed affluence. It is a
sociological truism that leisure classes since time immemorial
have cloaked economically unproductive or even exploitative
positions in society with claims to esoteric insight or cultural
seigniorality. But what remains remarkable in the 60's is that
so many proponents of the counterculture, even while learning
the Marxist analysis of wealth and its influence on human
thinking, could not recognize the social sources of their
own ideas.

A clue to the materialistic premises of popular liberal
theology was the manner in which it made a fetish out of altering
people's "consciousness." Now "Consciousness-raising" has
been a stock strategy of modern revolutionary theory. The
assumption has been that you have to make people keenly aware
of *why* they are the way they are before you can induce them
to act in a revolutionary fashion. On the other hand, the technique
of raising consciousness may also degenerate into a method
of propaganda to get people to believe something about themselves
which seems novel and exciting, but which in actuality does not
transform their real situation. When the key words in the
slogans of a revolutionary group lose their precise coinage and
tend to glitter for their own sake, then consciousness-raising
turns into manipulation and deception. Genuine consciousness-raising
makes people sharply conscious of something in their

lives which is wrong and needs reform. The counterculture, though, tended to drop "raising" and speak roundly only of "consciousness" itself, as if that were the magical elixir for salvation.

A best-selling book with a contagious theme in this vein was Charles Reich's *The Greening of America*, which came out in 1970. Reich trumpeted the advent of what he called "Consciousness Three," a new form of total awareness which had seized the young people and their imitators in the past decade. Consciousness Three was supposed to replace the first two stages of consciousness, the angles of vision our fathers and grandfathers had adopted toward the world. Consciousness Three did not imply consciousness of anything in particular. It was something akin to a wide-open and multi-sensory involvement in all of experience regardless of its meaning or context. Reich gave the quite mundane illustration of a student absorbed in rock music playing from his stereo system; or as Reich framed the issue a bit tritely, it was "the recovery of the self" in the innocence and primacy of raw experience. "To 'blow one's mind' means to become more aware."[6] In other words, the higher consciousness which Reich praised was merely a sort of retreat into the interior freedom and gratification of what goes on in the private sphere or in the pleasures of one's own head.

Consciousness Three became a veiled synonym for narcissism -- treating one's own subject fantasies and reveries as if they had a decisive social importance. One could be "conscious" without having to trouble oneself about the consequences of one's life-style within a larger matrix of social responsibilities. Actually, Consciousness Three demanded privilege and affluence for its support, as Reich himself rather *unselfconsciously* hinted.

> The new consciousness seeks new ways to live in light of what technology has made possible and desirable. Since machines can produce enough food and shelter for all, why should not man end the

> antagonism derived from scarcity and base his
> society on love for his fellow man? If machines
> can take care of our material wants, why should
> not man develop the aesthetic and spiritual side
> of his nature.7

Reich regarded material sufficiency as no longer a challenge to man. The possession of physical resources by the few, so that they may be free for "aesthetic and spiritual" pursuits, is construed as universally applicable to all, although it was not true even in the 60's that all members of modern society had reached the level of superfluous prosperity envisaged by Reich as the portal to utopia. The free-spirited and contemplative existence that Reich esteemed could be enjoyed mainly by those with access to wealth. Such wealth, if it had ever been equitably distributed, would not have seemed so abundant and so easy to take for granted; liberals no longer have imagined so many opportunities to remain indifferent to its procurement.

Consciousness Three was an open invitation to the affluent to dull themselves to the social dilemmas of wealth. Consciousness Three placed major stress on "experience," but it was the experience of rock concerts, marijuana "highs," or new sexual encounters, rather than the experience of getting one's daily bread. It meant that the appreciably well-off could skylark in the ecstasies of the moment while not having to be concerned about who washed their socks or labored at poverty wages to pick the food for their table. A wasteful but affluent economy churned out a surplus of riches for the many, thereby nurturing the illusion that scarcity and the need for productive human labor would never again constitute a challenge.

A vivid illustration of popular liberal theology's blindness to the dilemma of affluence was the so-called "theology of play," with which even the international dean of "political" and "liberation theology," Jürgen Moltmann, joined forces.8

The fact that Moltmann could make the breezy transition at the end of the last decade from the rhetoric of political revolution in his *Theology of Hope* to a solemnization of human festivity and play provides a good case study in the roots of liberal theology during this era.

The "theology of play" took its cue from the historical profile of *homo ludens* first proferred by Johann Huizinga. In 1955, in his book *Homo Ludens*, Huizinga attempted to subvert the modern technocratic image of man as *homo faber* ("man the toolmaker") by arguing for the importance of play, fantasy, and festivity in the origins of human culture.[9]

Huizinga's ideas lay fallow in theological circles for some time until Harvey Cox immortalized them in *The Feast of Fools*, proclaimed by many reviewers as a stunning about-face from his glamorization of man's worldly and political vocations in *The Secular City*. Cox wrote:

> "Without fantasy a society cuts itself off from the visceral fronts of renewal. Like individuals, civilizations repudiate them. They must learn to live with them creatively... An alternation is needed, and fantasy provides the bridge."[10]

Until this day Cox has not conceded having made any radical switch in his thinking, which implies perhaps that the theology of secular revolution is not as serious a business as many of the old-guard, fearing a sellout of faith to activist politics, may have presumed.

Following Cox's book there appeared a rather erudite exposition of the new theme by David Miller in his *Gods and Games*.[11] Miller made no significant effort to work the theology of play into a political agenda. His more likely audience was the urbane aesthetes of the religious academy as well as the lay readers of Tolkien and Peanuts. Then came Moltmann, whose latest opus made no great impression on American readers, probably because it was difficult to accept the dalliance of heavy Germanic theology with such a light-minded genre.

The theology of play conveyed a remarkably simple message: Christian thinkers should renounce trafficking with the rational and secular gods of social theory. The reason was not that social concerns were dead issues. The theology of play never disowned secular interests for the church. Instead it suggested that the theology transcend such interest. Theology should stop taking both itself and the moralistic programs of its worldly evangelists so seriously. It should celebrate the moments of playful abandon which all people experience, wherein the tragedies and tribulations of life, regardless of who is responsible for them, are overcome in a creative affirmation of one's own dreams and fantasies. The *real* "good news" of Christianity is that God does not condemn good "fun," but allows for play as a mode of reconciliation with the horrors of existence. *In The Feast of Fools* the picture of Jesus as the scarred "man" of sorrow with his crown of thorns is alchemized into "Christ the harlequin," the eternal jester and clown.

Such stuff was an indirect slap at the early death-of-God boys as well as at Bonhoeffer who celebrated pain and suffering, the modern *via dolorosa*, as the chosen life-style for Christians in the age of Auschwitz and Vietnam. Liberal culture has never seen any lasting virtue in suffering for its own sake, or even as a badge of faith, and it was not unexpected that such a metaphor would be replaced by the image of the carefree buffoon. As a reflection of American cultural history, Cox's "conversion" may be viewed against the backdrop of the passage from the civil rights marches and the first solemn war protests, to the coalescence of the hippie culture with its outrageous banter, street stunts, and satirical baiting of the establishment epitomized in Abby Hoffman's slogan, "revolution for the hell of it." The counterculture's rendition of revolution as a raunchy carouse in Central Park -- the ushering in of the social millenium by tribal rite was projected into the "theology of play."

The pseudo-primitivism of the counterculture later found expression in Cox's preoccupation with the colorful and dramatic festivals of rural Third World peoples. The theology of play sought to borrow the Mardi Gras spirit -- to make it a paradigm of liberation for rootless American urbanites, translating the sacred gestures of native rituals for the benefit of the capering adolescent mentality. The only drawback was that the theology of play took "play" too seriously and wanted to represent it as something more than everybody's natural disposition to let his hair down and act like children. Primitive culture has ritually institutionalized play and fantasy as a kind of psychic safety-valve for peoples immersed daily in the struggle for survival; the theology of play endeavored to make such antics a style of regular involvement. Primitive culture has legitimated play as a respite from labor and the burdens of practical morality; the theology of play aimed to make it a full substitute for work and practical morality. It rested on the release from toil presumably available to all who shared the blessings of affluence.

Cox, of course, has never tried to shuck the moral weight of his Baptist upbringing, and for that reason the pure gospel of play could never crowd out his commitment to social justice. The accomodation of social responsibility to the glad tidings of playful freedom, a task Cox sincerely strove to fulfill, was never convincingly carried through in his thought. Behind his claim in *The Feast of Fools* that play and fantasizing could furnish a constructive alternative to mere politics lurked the possibility that such a course might ultimately result in a kind of escapism. The theology of play, lacking strict safeguards, might well turn, as it probably did for those who read Miller, into a sophisticated opiate for the affluent. In his later work, *The Seduction of the Spirit*, Cox aimed to redress the balance.

The Seduction of the Spirit, appearing in 1973 when the counterculture was waning in its contribution to American life, toned down many improper implications which could have been drawn from *The Feast of Fools*. An index to the new temper of Cox's thinking was the manner in which he regarded his experiences at Esalen Institute, the center of the "sensitivity" movement. There emphasis on the free expression of bodily feeling and emotion as well as on mystical ecstasy put into practice many of the theoretical tenets of the theology of play. As a matter of protocol, Cox remarked favorably on his voyage through sensuous immediacy -- a "naked revival" was the way he characterized the process of initiation into group nudity, sybaritic massages, and the pervasive aroma of incense. Cox observed, again not to sound too disaffected with his seductive form of programmed transcendence, that "the sickness of our time is not the movement toward interiority but the disappearance of it."[12] However, he quickly added this warning:

> The whole group movement teaches that personal interiority cannot become actual without some supportive web of relationships. What we do not see, however, is that a world where greed reigns and people are set against one another by racial, sexual and hierarchical roles cannot provide such a web. Such a world twists this fragile net into distorting nooses. When the group adjourns, life is still choked instead of linked with the big world outside. Subjectivity can only emerge in a community of subjects, but we now inhabit deformed communities that produce deformed persons. We need a new web.[13]

The "supportive web of relationships" which Cox yearned for was exactly an antidote to privatism and the faddish immersal in exotic experiences that had stalked popular liberal theology. Cox was calling at long last for the recreation of a *community* of the spirit in which people struggled soberly and unpretentiously with their problems, helped each other out when need arose, and faced squarely sin and injustice. Furthermore, Cox

downplayed many of the frothy utopias of the counterculture
while evincing a nostalgia for the simple, middle-class culture
of small town America in which he had grown up. Malvern, Pennsylvania, that homely symbol of a stable folk culture which the
liberals of the 60's had damned as the hothouse of puritanism,
super-patriotism, and provincialism, -- of everything wrong with
the United States, now came in for reverent approval, if only
with stated reservations. In *The Seduction of the Spirit* Cox
compared Malvern's pious churchgoers to traditional religious
communities throughout the world. Cox was summoning back the
rootless, wearily experimental and overheated liberal imagination, to participation once again in the pre-industrial or
pre-affluent conditions of existence.

It was a howler, though, when Cox tended to confuse this
return to earth with the heady aspirations of the 60's. Remarkably, he talked of going back to the simpler life as
another instance of "liberation" in the *avant-garde* sense, as
another exercise for "radical theology." The analogy even
became absurd at one point when Cox averred:

> Though they might appear to differ from each
> other, the folk religion of a Pueblo village or a
> saint's day parade in an Italian section of New
> York City have much in common with a novem rock
> Mass celebrated by a group about to go on a peace
> march.[14]

The sentiment was about as far fetched as that of the eighteenth
century European noblewomen who in a pathetic attempt to put on
the identity of their impoverished subjects, had sumptuous little
garden houses built for them on the grounds of their estates to
which they snuck away unnoticed to be make-believe shepherdesses. Cox still clung somehow to the illusion that the
counterculture was innocent of its special prerogatives of
affluence -- that it was merely another embodiment of folkishness. The tenor of *The Seduction of the Spirit* reminds one of

the feudal Russian prince who visits a peasant church, buys two
or three icons from the priest, then returns to install them in
his private chapel while remaining a prince without a living
religion of his own. Similarly, the affluent romantically
assume the style of the underprivileged as though it were genuinely their own.

The Limits of Action

The familiar face of popular liberal theology has been
its devotion to activism. The theology of play, appearing
at the close of the 60's, perhaps reflected the frustration
of liberal politics in the church as an effective counter-
thrust to the government's Vietnam War policies and the
indifference of American society. The celebration of
uninhibited personal freedom and spontaneity became the
last reserve of meaningful protest against the system,
which gradually came to be perceived as evil less for its
political rigidity than for its suppression of creativity
and vital emotion. After all, Vietnam was not a "class"
war, as the self-styled Marxists in their fidelity to
left-wing political orthodoxy kept insisting; it was a
war at first generally supported by the working classes.
Those with a lesser stake in the affluent society --
factory workers, cab drivers, office clerks, small farm-
ers -- were those most inclined to rally to the defense
of the Johnson and Nixon Administrations against what they
perceived as a menace to their own values and loyalties.

For the liberal mind the immorality of the war did
not relate directly so much to social and economic issues
as it did to political and humanitarian ones. Liberal
activism took as its target the threats to political
freedom and conscience inherent in the draft, in the
stifling of campus protests, and in Nixon's and Agnew's

attempts to discredit or muzzle the media. The traditional socialists, of course, played up the economic meaning of the Vietnam War, but the abstruse and doctrinaire character of their analysis caught only scattered attention. Political activism, especially in the churches, was a series of *ad hoc* responses to special issues. When its undertakings made little headway, the natural inclination of liberals was to fall back into a way of asserting themselves only they could take -- exalt the joyous "experience" of contending with the principalities and powers of the world. Among liberals activism gradually declined into quietism, and withdrawal into subjectivity was proclaimed as the supreme duty of the alienated personality.

The reason for the failure of liberal activism, however, had little to do with activism itself. The failure can be attributed to the liberal's lack of any clear-cut reason for his engagement with the forces of society other than that of the Vietnam horror. It disrupted his life directly. In *The Secular City* Cox spoke glowingly of the church as "God's avant-garde" through which "committed" Christians try to identify "where the action is." Cox talked about liberating blacks, poor whites, Puerto Ricans, and other oppressed minorities (the day of women's liberation had not arrived) in a grand symphony of social concern. In this respect he simply gave ecclesiastical respectability to the programs of the Kennedy years. As political hostilities sharpened as the 60's wore on, and the intransigency of the power structure seemed more acute, popular liberal theology began to discern more devils to be exorcised while it tightened the definition of who was oppressed and why. The forms of oppression came to be conceived as ever more insidious and subtle. The central Washington agencies in which the activists of the early 60's had trusted were now typecast as the "enemy" and "part of the problem." Racism no longer was merely the fault of bad breeding of individuals; it was systemic and "institutional."

Such refinement of the nature of activist struggle echoed the feeling of betrayal experienced by many democrats under the Johnson Administration, which doled out Great Society money on the one hand and hiked the draft calls month after month on the other. At the same time the civil rights movement became the black power movement while the white liberal/black liberation alliance floundered. Then came the women's movement, creating further division even within the other spinoffs. Ethnicity and sex eclipsed the more global interests of the earlier 60's. Many liberals, lacking a meaningful area of action in which they themselves could participate, embraced the plight of the Third World peoples, who were, significantly too removed from the circus of American protest movements to care about the concerns of theology professors in Boston. It was an intriguing commentary that most of the contact between liberal churchmen and the Third World was through Third World Churchmen, who had often been trained in or associated with American theological seminaries.

The hackneyed conservative accusation against liberal activism was that it was nothing more than a continuous kind of half-hearted political therapy for assuaging deep-seated guilt feelings. Liberals, of course, have always thrived on guilt, but that was not the problem. There was indeed a real need for Americans to feel guilty about the manner in which they had consciously or inadvertently treated their own brethren as well as the disfranchized peoples of the world. In patronizing liberal guilt conservatives were tacitly admitting that they saw no reason to feel guilty, which was even worse.

The problem arose with the personal irrelevance to liberals of the causes to which they were contributing

money, moral support, and sometimes even jail sentences.
"Liberation theology" had its beginning with protests of
oppression made by certain spokesmen for the underdogs
in their first stabs at "black theology," "Latin American
theology," etc. But establishment liberal theologians
could not sincerely cite their own oppression, mainly because
they were hardly oppressed in real life. Most of them had
not even done time in prison for their political activism.
Exceptions were the Berrigans, and the few who had suffered
three-night detentions in Southern jails during the freedom-
rider campaigns. By the same token, attacks of liberal
theologians on economic misery were not certified by financial insolvency of their own. Popular liberal theology
had to experience oppression vicariously.

Women liberal theologians lit upon the bane of sexism.
It seemed a plausible *cause célèbre* because of role and job
discrimination affecting even Radcliffe graduates. The
trouble was that feminist theology tended to magnify this
not insignificant cultural issue by protraying it as a
political and economic one, while at the same time they
ignored the privileges of affluence that women, like men,
can both exploit and enjoy. Few feminist theologians had
ever been beaten, killed, or imprisoned for asserting
their rights within male culture, still they saw no
problem in blurring role subordination with actual
brutalization. The white male liberal, of course,
could not find a similar analogy in his own experience;
so he too tended to leap on the bandwagon of feminism
vicariously.

"Liberation theology," into which the activist theme
in religious liberalism finally developed, after a while
grew more and more imprecise about what liberation entailed.
The rudderless quality of liberal theology has always
allowed it to attack traditional social assumptions and

meanings mainly because it is more "original" to find fault with time-tested beliefs and customs than to renovate them. Hence liberation theology continued the process of social criticism for its own sake, bludgeoning new beliefs and customs and detecting in old ones further insidious forces. That is not to say that liberation theology was not correct in its exposure of both social wrongs and the bankruptcy of certain institutions. The rub was that it gradually lost the ability to make qualitative distinctions where required. For example, liberation theology suggested that all who mobilized under the flag of resisting "oppression" were to be embraced as comrades-in-arms. Theoretically, this stance could have justified support for both the Palestine Liberation Organization (PLO) and the Jewish Defense League, but that sort of hypothetical irony was never perceived.

Again Harvey Cox, who at one time or another in his career has mirrored just about all the competing popular theologies without covenanting with any particular one, gave voice to the liberationist imperative of getting into everybody's oppression.

> I raise my glass of tequila to that mural in Santa Fe, to the Mexican people whose gods and heroes it depicts, to the story of faith and struggle it tells. I know that in one sense it is "their" story, not mine. I will have to find or forge my own community. I cannot piggyback on theirs. I even realize with sadness that those against whom Zapata and Torres fought were in some sense "my" people. But still I lift my glass to their story and I know the toast is right, because at a deeper level, one we all can glimpse on occasion, "their" story is my story, too.[15]

The allusion of drinking a toast to a painting as a paradigm of political involvement is only a little amusing, though I am sure Cox did not intend it to be. His is the wistful plaint of the outsider who would really like to be a revolutionary of some kind. The poetic and romantic appropriation of "their story" as "my story too" involves a vicarious identification with suffering which could probably not be described so volubly were it a real presence in Cox's life. But Cox has never grasped the contradiction between sounding the muddled reveille of liberation for every conceivable contest, and *doing* something that makes sense within one's own situation. For all his disparagement of academic theology as too cerebral and not sufficiently activist, Cox has never himself been a real activist precisely because his activism has always remained abstract.

The contradiction is evident in a short piece Cox published in *The Christianity and Crisis Symposium*. "I believe it is time for 'theologians,'" Cox declares, "to stop *calling* for a North American theology of liberation and begin doing it." In the next sentence, however, he waffles on just what "doing it" entails. "This means *learning* [italics mine] from blacks, women, and Latin Americans that theology comes to life when it becomes the critical theory of church and religion."[16] In other words, liberation theology is just another method of theoretical identification (i.e., "learning") with the whole household of the oppressed. The other side of the coin is "critical theory," in which popular liberal theology has always delighted. "For Americans this means theology becomes the muckraker, ideology-exposer, cliché uncoverer, and demystifier of corporate capitalism."[17]

Now upending the ideology of corporate capitalism is perhaps the paramount task for all Americans today who reel in their personal lives from the depredations of an economic system which has outlived its usefulness. Indeed, it probably should be inscribed in the charter of theology, though God forbid that the next years see the gestation of a "theology of populism." On the other hand, Cox in this testimony wants to make the ravages of corporate capitalism just another item on the unwieldy agenda of a diffuse liberation theology. "Blacks, women, and Latin Americans" -- the goal becomes more and more hazy. Little of the serious thinking needed in a true "critical theory" is possible in such a context. Again the diffuseness of liberal theology seems inevitable when the absence of a viable social or religious identity epidemic among today's academic elite hampers the formation of theological objectives. "Liberation for the hell of it," to amend slightly Abby Hoffman's dictum, may be a slight distortion of Cox's position, but it nevertheless bears some notable affinity with it.

There has been a stirring within the camp of liberation theology, though, to describe the situation. Rosemary Ruether, perhaps the most earnest and least pretentious of liberation theologians, has pointed it out forcefully. Ruether writes that the "mediating role" of theologians who sympathize with the oppressed yet who do not share their oppression

> becomes aborted when the "alienated intelligentsia" becomes concerned primarily with its own self-purification through disaffiliation with its own class or nation: when it seeks primarily a parasitic identification with the oppressed who are viewed, idealistically, as the "suffering saviors," who can do no wrong or in whom all is to be excused.[18]

Ruether would prefer instead that liberation theology perform apostolic service to its own community, demonstrating to it its culpability and summoning it to repentance. Such of course, was what the Black Panthers asked of conscientious white radicals instead of their servilely trying to play the role of blacks themselves. On the other hand, the "mediation" for which Ruether calls remains impossible so long as those in favor of liberation have no common ground with both sides of the confrontation. The tragedy of popular liberal theology

is that it has sought, albeit romantically, to distance itself
from normative culture while losing just about all touch with
its own people with whom it may want, as an afterthought, to
be reconciled. Both poverty and privilege have produced their
own outcasts, and neither has allowed for an empathetic understanding of the majority in the middle, should genuine
"mediation" ever get off the ground.

It may well be that some liberationists, who never drank
the full cup of alienation, will learn the art of mediation.
Certainly one such instance of the wayward son come home is
the theologian and now social commentator, Michael Novak.
Novak, who has been one of the most prolific of popular liberal
theologians, gained fame in the 60's as a Catholic partisan of
liberation notions. In his *A Theology for Radical Politics*
(1969) he recited within the framework of Catholic social
thinking the liturgy of the "movement." A few years later,
however, in 1972, he raised a few eyebrows in liberal circles
when he unexpectedly made a plea for sympathy toward the lifestyles and world-view of the "hard hat," flag-waving philistines
in his book *The Unmeltable Ethnics*. Novak renounced the liberal
jeremiad against the middle classes and conventional morals in
favor of a sympathetic portrait of their humble, if not benighted, parochialism. In a companion work, *Book of Elements*,
published in the same year, and even more of a contrite testimonial to his apostasy from his middle-class roots, Novak went
beyond the idyll of working class ethnicity that he had long
outgrown, and gave voice to the pathos of his living as a
successful college professor and literary celebrity whose
authentic concerns in life are his family, his garden, and his
suburban home on Long Island. *Book of Elements* comprised a
lyrical collage of diary, monologue, and impromptu poetry --
all a self-conscious and unaffected confession of the limitations
of being liberal.

"No one ever told me caring for an old home could be such fun."[19]

"Is it wrong to love to work in the garden? Dreadfully suburban. Intellectual friends visit and notice that we have a stationwagon, bushes from the nursery poking out the windows, a red wheelbarrow in the yard. How can I explain?"[20]

"It is, I know, shameless to have a home, television, time for lawns and sports, and beer ...shameless in a world of poverty and misery... or else...or else perhaps not so. More crucial by far to find contentment, to be at peace. It is not inner peace that breeds the evils of the world but restlessness...I wish I could convince myself of that."[21]

The pitch of these confessions sounds mournfully privatistic -- privatism without the charade of being something else. Yet Novak recognizes the dangers of the modern American form of privatism -- its excessive individuality, its obsession with leisure, power, and wealth. There is only the modest recognition that man must cultivate and enrich what is at hand, rather than tilt all the time with the metaphysical windmills of evil, or fill his soul with visions of dragons and new calls to chivalry. It is the theme of "tilling our own garden" on which Voltaire embroiders at the end of *Candide*. Novak resists the privative lure by resurrecting from the grave of countercultural scorn the idea of "connectedness" -- the durable loyalty to family, friends, the immediate community, which is something more than a boisterous hippie "love fest" on a Sunday afternoon.

Novak's Catholic rearing may have a lot to do with this mood, but it represents a yearning that toward the end of the 70's may well-up within the hearts of many Americans, particularly the popular liberal claques. After all, did not Bob Dylan turn family-man and homebody even before the dust of the 60's had settled? Dylan's hermitage may have signalled, not his betrayal of the "revolution," but his domestication of it. The end of the age of affluence may clip considerably many of the luxuries and civilities, like a suburban home which Novak rhapsodizes about. On the other hand, the dwindling of superfluous wealth and the mobile, sensationalist, and streamlined life-style which has gone with it may encourage the revival of workaday pursuits and values. That change of circumstances, even more than the end of the Vietnam War and the exhaustion of radical politics, may facilitate a liberal homecoming to the soil of common experience -- arousal of new interest in refashioning a community of persons who struggle with the unromantic problems of changing diapers, keeping the slugs away from the azaleas, and fighting city-hall when need be. An activism once highly volatile, individualistic, eclectic, apocalyptic, and short-lived, may give way to working within given community structures to *rehabilitate those structures* within the limits of the possible. Liberal activism may come home from Brazil, Mexico, and the black ghetto to make over Muncie once again.

That is not to say that we must acquiesce to the forces of reaction, bigotry, and political chicanery. The irony of today is that while traditional liberal activism has become flat and sometimes despairing, the traditional bearers of middle-class culture have begun to reaffirm and take responsibility for their lives. Popular liberal theology, in particular, was never that "popular." It created fantasies for those who, for various reasons, Vietnam included, wanted to pull exotic masks over their faces while refusing to recognize who they really were. It wanted to build a culture on social irresponsibility, instability, and isolation (the "generation gap" and the cult of youth were neon signs of this condition) which affluence had produced. The liberal fantasies began to fade as soon as hard times hit, while the new message seemed to be that of Wadsworth:

> Not in utopia -- subterranean fields, --
> Or some secreted island, Heaven knows where!
> But in the very world, which is the world
> Of all of us, -- the place where, in the end
> We find our happiness, or not at all!
>
> *The Prelude* bk.x. 1:140

The ideology of affluence, however, identified the "world" with the various forms of high-living, and "happiness" with the privatized ethic of self-actualization. This popular liberal theology digested without ever blushing but in doing so sold its soul to the devil in contemporary culture. A paradox lay in what we go on to consider -- that popular liberal theology preached the salvation of the individual, while disregarding the meaning and worth of *persons*.

NOTES TO CHAPTER 2

1. "Whatever Happened to Theology?" *Christianity & Crisis* (May 12, 1975) 35:112-17.

2. cf. Sam Keen, "Manifesto for a Dionysian Theology," in Herbert Richardson and Donald Cutler, *Transcendence* (Boston: Beacon Press, 1968).

3. David Miller, *The New Polytheism* (New York: Harper & Row, 1974).

4. Norman Vincent Peale, *The Power of Positive Thinking* (Greenwich: Fawcett, 1969).

5. Donald Meyer, *The Positive Thinkers* (Garden City: Doubleday, 1965).

6. Charles Reich, *The Greening of America* (New York: Random House, 1970), p. 276.

7. Reich, p. 353.

8. cf. Jürgen Moltmann, *The Theology of Play* (New York: Harper & Row, 1972).

9. cf. Johann Huizinga, *Homo Ludens* (Boston: Beacon Press, 1955).

10. Harvey Cox, *The Feast of Fools* (New York: Harper & Row, 1969), p. 69

11. David Miller, *Gods and Games* (New York: Harper & Row, 1972).

12. Harvey Cox, *The Seduction of the Spirit* (New York: Simon & Schuster, 1973), p. 222.

13. Cox, p. 223.

14. Cox, p. 167.

15. Cox, p. 257

16. "Whatever Happened to Theology?" p. 115.

17. Ibid.

18. Rosemary Ruether, *Liberation Theology* (New York: Paulist Press, 1972), p. 14.

19. Michael and Karen Novak, *A Book of Elements* (New York: Herder & Herder, 1972), p. 4.

20. Novak, p. 106.

21. Novak, p. 108.

CHAPTER 3

The Dark Night of the Person

> "I claim no country
> for peace is my land
> I claim no saviour
> for love is my salvation
> I claim no family
> for all mankind is my brother"[1]

The Landscape of Homelessness

The above lines, simple and perhaps trite, were written by a student poet in commemoration of a war protest that took place on a Colorado university campus during the spring of 1970 in the aftermath of the Cambodian invasion. At first glance they merely evoke the stock sentiments of the anti-war movement and the youth culture along with the appropriate catchwords: peace, love, brotherhood. Yet their context is less important than their revelation of emerging social values. Juxtaposed with celebration of high-minded and humanistic ideals which the youth culture made its own is a throughgoing skepticism about the worth of all familiar institutions and moral attitudes. The young poet "claims" no country, no family, no redeemer, that is, no specific and familiar objects of allegiance in which to invest her energies. Instead she puts her faith as a liberated soul in misty abstractions which supposedly compensate for her abandonment of traditional ties. She has cast herself as a vagabond of the universal spirit, identifying in a kind of emotional and mystical rapture with nothing and everything, with no place and every place, with no lover except love itself.

The eminent psychoanalyst, Erik Erikson, has written of the tendency in all adolescents to wrest themselves free for a time from the definitions of the world and the image of themselves nurtured in their minds by parents and society during the long years of growing up. Such is the stuff of adolescent rebellion, in which atheism, iconococlasm, and experiments are psychologically valuable rites of passage from the uncritical conformity of childhood to the autonomy of adulthood. There is always a tendency, Erikson observes, for people to find emancipation from conventional ideas and morality rather dizzying and frightening. Hence, they move from an instinctive attachment to familial or tribal norms to an intoxicated embrace of grand causes. Having lost all feeling for particular goals, they acquire a "cosmic identity" -- a diffuse sense of participation in all of existence. Erikson calls this phase of psychic development "totalism," and describes it as follows:

> We must postulate...a psychological need for totality without further choice or alteration... When the human being, because of accidental or developmental shifts, loses an essential wholeness, he restructures himself and the world by taking recourse to what we may call *totalism*.[2]

The "natural" disposition of youth to solve the identity crisis of late childhood in this manner, however, seems to have been both reinforced and distorted by the experience of the 60's. Then the Vietnam War brought into sharp focus the incipient decadence, real or imagined, of American values and social practices.

It has always been the habit of youth to call to account the professions and commitments of their elders, posing some kind of alternative system of meaning to which they can wholeheartedly subscribe. In the long haul, though, the "wisdom" of the older generation is affirmed. Mark Twain quipped that over

the years he had discovered that his father seemed to have grown
a lot "smarter!" Yet the 60's closed off for many rebellious
youth this eventual reconciliation. The authority of elders
struck them not only as adverse, but also as "hypocritical" and
hollow. In other words, the wisdom of the older generation was
condemned by rebellious youth not just "foolish" or benighted
but as a *lie*. Among many aging veterans of the last decade,
that condemnation gave way not to cynicism about all values and
institutions. The Watergate affair and the fall of Richard
Nixon only deepened the disaffection.

For the most part, therefore, the "totalism" of recent
youthful protest has been compounded of a vast sense of the
emptiness of modern cultural forms, and a loss of sound moorings
to which youth could eventually hitch their lives. This has
been the by-product of burgeoning affluence. The connecting
of affluence with the disintegration of family, community
groups, and national loyalties has been, over the years, something of a sociological cliché. Yet its familiarity does not
subtract from its importance. As we discussed earlier, the
creation of the affluent society has depended largely on the
division of units, manipulative and expendable, in order to
maximize the flow of goods and services, and therefore, the
efficiency of the process. Heads of families are sundered from
lasting neighborhood and community ties so that they can become
better "performers" on the job; they do not compromise their
fealty to the organization for which they work by their commitments to other organizations. The nineteenth century "company
town," designed by the capitalist entrepreneur to incorporate
the social needs of his employees into the rigid demands of
factory routine, has been succeeded by the sprawling suburb or
"bedroom community" beyond which work, done far away and beyond
the area of communal responsibility, becomes the only meaningful
pursuit for millions of Americans. The fabric of family life,

in the past interwoven with other parochial and civic involvements, has gradually been displaced by its current form, encompassing the phenomenon of the lonely "corporate" wife, or its emerging counterpart -- the career woman with just as little time or concern for domestic affairs as the employed man. No wonder, then, that the task of identity formation for the young has become so difficult.

With stable institutional guides gone, the individual is thrown upon his own resources to discover who he is. But in a culture where the only real source of identification is one's work or mode of production, those resources are deficient for the task, and he takes on *pseudo-identities* through Walter Mitty fantasies, vicarious participation in the causes of oppressed peoples far removed from one's own immediate situation, attachment to artificial subcultures and movements such as "consciousness-raising" groups or motorcycle gangs. Such pseudo-identities, however, prove transitory and unsatisfying; they are quickly cast aside and replaced in serial fashion with all the nonchalance given to one-night stands. The much touted "freedom" of modern affluent existence easily becomes a complusive and unrelenting search for a solid framework of significance in which people can find their understanding of themselves. Such freedom entraps them in what the sociologist, Peter Berger, has called "the homeless mind."

The homeless mind, according to Berger, results from the withering of people's social and psychological roots in a culture which has lost its power to direct lives toward clear and permanent tasks and goals. In the past when some semblance of traditional morality and social expectations remained in force, individuals could gauge who they were and what they were likely to become in terms of prevailing norms or opportunities frequently given religious sanction. Thus, the child of an artisan looked forward to taking over the father's trade, or at least staying within the community of experience derived from that line of work, that is, his social class. Even in America, with its pluralism, social mobility, and egalitarian sentiments, there lingered cultural guideposts such as religion, family, and geographic region against which a person could measure himself. A person's "life world" was constituted by these factors which, though they may have barred him from entering any career, or from grooming himself for a particular style of living that seemed satisfying, yet made his "finding his niche" less chancy. Today, however, more and more guideposts are gone. Berger writes:

> Modern identity is *peculiarly open*. While undoubtedly there are certain features of the individual that are more or less permanently stabilized at the conclusion of primary socialization, the modern individual is nevertheless peculiarly "unfinished" as he enters adult life. Not only does there seem to be a great objective capacity for transformations of identity in later life, but there is also a subjective awareness and even readiness for such transformations. The modern individual is not only peculiarly "conversion-prone;" he knows this and often glorifies in it. Biography is thus apprehended both as a migration through different social worlds and as the successive realization of a number of possible identities.[3]

In earlier times social groups or institutions tended to claim some consistent loyalty from their members, not because they were excessively authoritarian, but because they afforded a sense of place -- a mental "home." The homelessness of the contemporary psychological nomad is dramatized in the general drift of people's attention from one fad to the next, from one fragile object of commitment to another. A cartoon in a national magazine, for instance, caricatured the dissolution of serious religious involvement in a way that would have seemed outlandish only a generation back. It showed one bearded youth glibly confiding to a second: "Right now I'm *between* religions." By the same token, the rising incidence of divorce, coupled with an equal tendency toward remarriage with or without children, suggests the twilight of even the most venerable context of personal identity -- the family. The erosion of family life has brought not the emancipation of the individual but a dull hunger for something deeper.

There has, of course, been no dearth of defenders for this state of affairs. It has become fashionable to celebrate the liberty of the homeless personality -- the homeless mind -- as a desirable alternative to the middle-class vision. The hidebound provincial has been an obsessive theme of American literature in this century, exemplified in Sinclair Lewis' novels of the 1920's as well as in the surreal, cinematic psychodrama, *Easy Rider*, which won the acclaim of youth in the late 60's and early 70's. In theology, Harvey Cox's *Secular City* was a sober testament favoring release from traditional social ties and identities as a gateway to the new "freedom." Cox declared that "urbanization" and the uprooting of historically prescribed roles and duties "can be seen as a liberation from some of the cloying bondage of preurban society... Urban man's deliverance from enforced convention makes it necessary to choose for himself. His being anonymous to most people permits him to have a face and a name for others."[4] A more updated version of Cox's encomium on urban humanity, with a *suburban* focus, is *The Radical Suburb*, by John Orr and Patrick Nichelson.[5] It lauds the experimentalism, sensuality, and even libertinism of "expansive man," who becomes the new norm for "revolutionary" society. In the popular lingo of youth, what social theorists and psychologists of the past have referred to benignly as "socialization" or "acculturation" is now translated liberally as "brainwashing." Much of the new "pop" psychotherapy seeks to abolish the "scripts" or "programs" "imposed" upon our consciousness in our growing up, and to encourage us to write our own life plans and policies entirely.

In short, the risks of establishing an identity in a world where signboards for personal meaning have disappeared or have been ridiculed into obscurity are taken as preferable to the old ways at any cost. The landscape of homelessness is glorified for its openness, not for its emptiness and bleakness. The homeless mind revels in the belief that it is a blank slate on which vast new experiences can be inscribed -- revels until it discovers that those experiences in the long run have little substance. The loss in common culture of common sources of personal identity provides only a hollow freedom without consolation.

The Dark Night of the Person

Perhaps the most enduring misconception of modern liberal culture has been the notion of the "person" as a purely indeterminate individual divested of the shackles of law, government, and peer pressure. Though rarely expanded into a doctrine of anarchism, the modern conception of personhood has come to suggest negative quality -- resistance of conformity in order to enjoy and cultivate one's own singularity. The Romantic era in Western intellectual history gave the word "person" the connotation of solitariness and uniqueness. Today we talk about "personalizing" everything from stationery to education, implying that the needs and even the pretenses of the ego take precedence over what other people say about or demand of us. "Personal" has overtones of moral or intellectual self-determination; it is frequently contrasted with the *impersonality* of "mass" culture and its effects on people's lives. In this connection "personal" is synonymous with "individual," which is less a term for distinguishing between physical entities, as in biology, than a term for making a general claim about who decides what is real or meaningful. Persons and society are seen in unrelenting conflict with each other.

The translation of the word "person" into the grammar of individualism, however, is a distinctively modern occurrence. In the Latin of early Christianity the term *persona* did not have to do with individuality *per se* so much as it did with social roles and rankings. In Roman law, a "person" was one accorded certain aristocratic titles and privileges by law; thus, a slave or foreigner, conceived as lacking them, had no "personality." To be a person often implied one's being favored in the administration of justice. That lies behind the King James' rendition of the passage in the New Testament where God is said to be "no respecter of persons" (Acts 10:43), a strange phrasing indeed for contemporary readers who expect the Bible to sound like the new individualist psychologies. Strictly speaking, a "person" was not a unique human being but a mask worn by an actor on stage to represent a character or function. Thus, when the Nicene Creed speaks of the three persons of the Godhead, it speaks of God, not as three separate individuals; it speaks of three manifestations of "aspects" of the divine.

A person was to be regarded chiefly as an instance of a greater type, as a particular illustration of something more than the bare individual. To be a person required full participation in a social and cultural order of life, while in the theological vein it involved a right relationship with one's Maker. Even in Protestant Christianity, which has made a sizable contribution religiously and historically to the modern notion of individualism, the teaching is explicit that a person is "nothing" apart from the transcendent power and grace that sustains him. Soren Kierkegaard, for example, in *The Sickness Unto Death*, came to the conclusion that while the single person may revolt against the "necessity" of social and biological existence in affirmation of his inherent freedom, he can realize that freedom only in communion with God. In fine, the recent notion of the person as a totally free individual, who needs no higher measure of his purpose or destiny, is remarkable and unprecedented.

The origin of the individualistic understanding of personhood lies with the industrial revolution and the growth of affluence. The Enlightenment, which devised its habits of thought in the light of the decline of feudal and aristocratic society and the rise of commercial civilization, stressed the notion of *personal liberty*. That entailed the dissolution of prescribed social obligations and the granting of rights to the individual to do whatever he considered rational, profitable, or prudent, particularly in economic transactions. "Personhood" thus incorporated ownership and enjoyment of property without interference from outside authorities. With John Locke, for example, humanity in "the state of liberty" allowed each individual "to dispose of his Person *or* Possession" in the manner he deems fit.[6] As an ethical principle this assumption is equivalent to the doctrine that in his moral life a person must be confronted with no obstacles to individual choice in most matters. He must have the "liberty" of "doing what one desires," as John Stuart Mill put it.

What has been missing in the liberal idea of personhood down to the modern period is any implication that personal identity must be tied up with social identity, or even with an ethic of corporate responsibility. The German anarchist and free-thinker of the nineteenth century, Max Stirner, summed up the abstract individualism of what he called "political liberalism" when he wrote:

> The freedom of man is, in political liberalism, freedom from *persons*, from personal dominion, from the *master*; the securing of each individual person against other persons, personal freedom.[7]

Here the category of personality was shorn of all positive
meaning and reduced to the notion of the insular individual
in competition with other individuals. Not only political
institutions, but also social institutions which seek to bind
human beings in a web of duties, were said to compromise the
autonomy of persons. The economic basis of this picture of
the human condition was, of course, the need for the accumulation of capital and the liberation of the lone entrepreneur
from government restrictions on his production of good. In
feudal society politics, morality, and religion were inextricably knitted together. In the new bourgeois society, economic
laissez-faire went hand in hand with exemption of one from
viewing the world in what once had been the commonly held way.

This negative freedom of the person left no standard of
individual worth other than what one reaped or accomplished
while romanticism sculptured an image of the person as a mosaic
of subjective experiences, popular culture shaped the ideal of
the "self-made man" who attains his standing in the eyes of his
fellows according to his wealth or prestige. The definition
of the person primarily in terms of property rather than of
social role drained the concept of person of all social content. By the same token, the person was no longer seen as an
integral expression of culture, or of the natural order, or
of the divine harmony of life; the person was simply a mechanism
in the productive process. Marx talked about capitalism converting people into *commodities* who could be exchanged like
nails and soap on the open market.

But the situation is further to be explained. The spread
of affluence and the mounting pace of social change stimulated
by it rendered impossible the preservation or even the
formation of reliable institutions or customs in respect to
which the questions "Who am I?" or "What am I to do?" could
be given credible answers. In assigning the blame, critics

of the modern world have ritualistically branded technology as
the villain to blame for the "dehumanization" of the social
environment. By "dehumanization" is usually meant *depersonalization*, the erosion of respect for the dignity and value of
individual personalities. Actually, the depersonalizing process
has come about, paradoxically, with the increased concern of
modern culture *for* the individual. And the fault has not been
technology, which only in the mid-twentieth century has been
increasingly perceived as a colossal menace, notwithstanding
the Romantics' horror of the "dark Satanic mills" of large-
scale industry. Technology has developed merely as a massive
engine for Western humanity's drive toward allaying economic
scarcity and promoting general wealth. The reason for the
sclipse of the person lies with the subordination of all human
goals and ambitions to the expansion of prosperity at the
expense of more enduring elements in the quality of life.

The cause if not some vague preference for material goods
over "spiritual" ones -- human beings have always had a
materialistic bent insofar as they strive for physical security.
The cause is the means by which material sufficiency has been
achieved. For as said earlier, the pursuit of affluence has
required the transformation of human beings not only into mere
agents of production, but also into interchangeable components
of an efficient system which easily become obsolete when
changes take place. The tendency of liberal political thought
to atomize social institutions and to think of the person
apart from his role in community has helped to rationalize
this transformation. Further, the dealing of liberal political
thought with the issue of technology without analyzing carefully the social values which put human beings into the service
of the machine has obscured the real causes of the current
crisis. The push toward affluence has fostered the mood of
social isolation and the lack of personal accountability. The

priority of the individual over the social body has left him prey to the manipulative forces of industrial technology and the totalitarian state. Such was the consequence of the political absolutism of the sixteenth century which broke the power of the medieval guilds and the influence of the church, leaving the individual victim, in his village, to mass regimentation by the nineteenth century industrial magnate. During the 1920's and 1930's Stalin realized that he could industrialize Russia and raise the general standard of living only by obliterating traditional social ties and groups, such as the rural peasant communes and the orthodox church. Soviet Communism's hostility to organized religion has been prompted less by theoretical atheism than by its recognition that such an institution competes with the demands of the state for maximum economic productivity.

In contemporary America the fundamental imperative of the affluent society toward ever-increased material productivity has been overlooked by those who fix their attention solely on social change. Social change with its loss of a secure footing for personal identity is frequently but wrongly regarded as some mysterious historical current that cannot be reversed or stopped. Alvin Toffler's *Future Shock*, a runaway best-seller in the early 1970's, incorporates such a fallacy. According to Toffler, today's technological and social changes have reached such staggering velocity that to seek their slowing down is futile. It is useless to moon for the good old days when the pace of life was much more temperate and people could more readily accommodate their beliefs and attitudes to change. The universal lesson is to run with the tide. Toffler accepts the loss of durability both in the consumer products we buy and in our family and social relationships as an unavoidable consequence of the times. Obsolescence in spouses

and jobs as well as in cars is a necessary concomitant of those
far-flung contemporary developments which Toffler suggest is
not as bad as they seem. In Toffler's words,

> Consciously or not, we define our relationships with most people in functional terms. So long as we do not become involved with the shoe salesman's problems at home...he is, for us, fully interchangeable with any other salesman of equal competence. In effect, we have applied the modular principle to human relationships. We have created the disposable person: Modular Man.[8]

Toffler obviously takes for granted in *Future Shock* the
perpetuation of economic growth and the steady enlargement
of individual wealth at all levels of society. Like many of
the popular theologians mentioned in the last chapter as well
as the various other apologists for Protean life-styles,
Toffler supposes that the tempo of personal living, present
and future, must be *allegro*, that an uninhibited zest for
travel, spending, and flitting from one social craze to the
next must occupy everyone from now on. The distinct bias of
the "beautiful people" who directly benefit from the spoils
of affluence appears throughout Toffler's writing. A magazine editor and media mogul seduced by the siren song of the
"gusto of living," he unwittingly refuses to acknowledge the
alienation inherent within the forms of thought and behavior
he praises. For him, the foundering of stable culture is a
token of the "new freedom," and he has no feel for the anxiety
and neurosis afflicting people caught in its stream. Traumatized by social change, they are diagnosed by Toffler as
suffering from "future shock," a syndrome of which they are
to be cured altering their perspectives rather than their
social circumstances. The therapy must apply to the patient
only. The disappearance of the integral personality possessing a genuine sense of belonging to an ordered universe if not
lamented; it is ratified as a facet of the new shape of things.

It is interesting, too, that in his second best-seller, *The Eco-Spasm Report*, which confronted the energy crisis and the prospect of diminished affluence, Toffler still embraced the ideology of rapid change. For him the end of affluence was merely another eddy in the whirlwind of contemporary history. On the other hand, Toffler did begin to take seriously the "ecology" of cultural and economic relationships thrown out of kilter by affluence, and the need to redress the balance in a future-shocked world. He observed:

> It is not the physical ecology alone that must be taken into account before we seize on any economic program for dealing with the crisis. There is, in addition, a "social ecology" that must be considered. For example, attempts to maintain high efficiency in industry by repeatedly relocating workers may bring with its stress, the death of communities, and other negative effects.
>
> The idea of a quick "economic fix" is just as dangerous as the comparable idea...that there is for each of our difficulties a neat, quick, "technological fix."[9]

The social ecology that Toffler called for, though, incorporates mainly artificial adjustments to an increasingly confused situation. For example, rather than proposing ways to rehabilitate the ever shrinking and fragmented family, Toffler drafted models of new work arrangements and government programs to make existing conditions more tolerable. The depersonalization of life in the affluent society will continue with the end of affluence, but it will be relieved by ingenious new methods of social manipulation, or what he called "crisis management." Toffler backed away from the brink of "1984," but the subtle implication he left was that an enviornment nurturing the growth of moral values and a sense of true personhood must be left behind by the new "superindustrialism."

Toffler underlined the failure of economic planning in working for the common welfare, and recognized the need for bringing into view the whole of human culture as well as the need for democratic participation. He ignores, however, the fact that any society can long sustain itself only if it evolves adequate symbols and ideals which supply deep meaning to personal existence. Thus "education for change," as Toffler describes it, or even the revived sensitivity of society's managers and functionaries to the complexity of the contemporary predicament, will not solve the problem. The end of affluence must also spell the end of reeling and destructive social change. The dark night of the person in modern society will only grow blacker unless our present culture is rescued from its excessive individualism, moral relativism, hedonism, and mania for the "new." It must be spared the perpetuation of a system which snaps vital connections between people and hurls them into the abyss of loneliness and uncertainty where they are subject to sinister and inhuman powers, whether they be the high priests of Mammon or the trustees of the totalitarian state.

Psycho-religiosity: The Opium of the Middle Classes

The early 1970's witnessed something of a "religious revival" different from the resurgence of organized religion after the Second World War. Its emphasis was generally on mysticism and experiential religion, with a leaning even in the Protestant churches toward the Oriental variety and its use of meditation techniques. In the past several years what used to be called "encounter groups" or "T-groups" have linked up with the new spirituality both inside and outside the churches to produce the so-called "Human Potential Movement." The practice of this movement has been bolstered with an infusion of popular psychologies including Arthur Janov's "primal stream therapy," Fritz Perl's "gestalt therapy," and "transactional analysis" pioneered by the late Eric Berne.

It would be no exaggeration to say that both the new religiosity and the Human Potential Movement tend to look to modern psychology as a path to salvation. The Human Potential Movement believes that the disquiet of the soul can be relieved through mastery of thoughts, impulses, and desires which may or may not be evident to consciousness. The aim is simply to "get one's head together," as the cliché goes. Self-examination aims to dispel obsessions, hang-ups, niggling feelings of frustration and anger, by fostering a new slant on "reality" within the psyche, to help people see in a novel and refreshing way what was for them a frightening or unpleasant world, all with the end of making them truly "happy." Similarly, many of the new therapies in the Human Potential Movement are directed toward lifting the burden of guilt and anxiety from which distressed moderns chronically suffer, and creating loving and happy individuals -- authentic "winners," to use the expression of Muriel James, a psychologist who has endeavored to apply transactional analysis within the church.[10]

Thus such psycho-religiosity, or the substitution of inward exploration for conventional religious sensibility seeks the "cure" of the disoriented human spirits that abound in the affluent society. The dominant credo of the new psycho-religiosity is that modern society has made sleepwalkers out of most people, suppressing their emotions and awareness of their own bodies. In place of passive and conditioned robots, the Human Potential Movement aims to turn out spontaneous, exuberantly self-conscious, and self-assured persons at one with their surroundings. As William Schutz, the author of *Joy* has commented, the point is to ensure a "fulfillment" which "brings to an individual the feeling that he can cope with his environment; the sense of confidence in himself as a significant, competent, lovable person who is capable of handling situations as they arise, able to use his own capacities, and free to express his feelings. Joy requires a vital, alive body, self-contentment, productive and satisfying relations with others, and a successful relation to society."[11]

In one crucial respect the new psycho-religiosity has endeavored to quench the thirst for personal identity and rewarding experience which have been denied by modern social arrangements. It urges people to cease striving to live up to sterile expectations of them, or to escape from unsatisfying roles or jobs. It calls upon them to rediscover who they really are. The new therapies, according to Jerome Liss, start with the premise that "people are unhappy," that the "average" individual in society is haunted by doubts about himself and about the purpose of his own life.[12] In response to the superficiality and hypocrisy of ordinary social dealings, the new therapies attempt to encourage frankness, self-expression, and empathy. In response to the absence of real community, they create circles of intimate and concerned fellow sufferers and confessors, which is what "encounter groups" are all about in theory. Through shared experience within the group compelling life meanings can emerge in a manner virtually impossible in people's workaday routines. The supportive presence of the group tends to relieve the bitter pangs of isolation and discontent and make the individual "feel good" for a time -- to dwell on the upbeat, to be able to say in the language of transactional analysis, "I'm OK, you're OK."

In essence, the new psycho-religiosity has for its agenda the restoration of the "whole person" in a torn and fragmented culture. John E. Biersdorf, director of the Institute for Advanced Pastoral Studies, has summed up the thrust of the Human Potential Movement, especially, in an article in *Christianity & Crisis*. The Human Potential Movement aims to maximize "personal growth," Bierdorf contends. Such "growth" consists chiefly in the enlargement of self-consciousness and the tapping of deeper feelings and fantsies nor recognized formerly by the individual as part of himself. The opening up of the frontiers of mind and body puts the individual in touch with a power or source of insight that transcends the finite consciousness yet animates the psyche and enhances the sense of personhood. As Biersdorf notes:

> The deep exploration of one's own inner space often leads to experiences which seem to be similar to those reported by followers of the great religious traditions. And interpersonal intimacy sometimes leads to intimacy of love and grace that, for want of a better words, have been called "transpersonal," i.e., inclusive of, but involving more than, the interpersonal other.[13]

Reclamation of the person, therefore, actually involves the abandonment of the singular ego with all its appetites, inclinations, and attachments to the free play of what Carl Jung termed the "collective unconscious," an impersonal life force expressed and individuated in the experiences of the personal self. For the most part, the way of redemption sought by the new psycho-religiosity verges on a mystical experience, with the exception that the initiate does not end up a lonely ascetic, nor does he attain to some permanent and all-inclusive *nirvana* state. Instead he goes back to living a normal life yet with a "higher" and fuller awareness of how his conscious thoughts and aspirations are only jutting promontories in a vast sea of unarticulated reality. He resolves the dilemma of personhood in a world without fixed indicators of identity by renouncing existing cultural forms of meaning and giving himself over to the dark and undisciplined energies of his subconscious, which he construes as somehow "cosmic."

It would be impossible here to go into all the different nuances and ramifications of the mystical or semi-mystical moods which the new psycho-religiosity promotes, or to survey the techniques and exercises whereby these moods are developed in the group setting. The question with which we are concerned is how people manage to order their lives in the wasteland of contemporary society. The new psycho-religiosity has been enthusiastically endorsed, particularly by many cultural pace-setters and a few liberal theologians, as an answer to the dilemmas of American life in mid-century that is supposedly superior to the aborted political activism of the 60's. Biersdorf has labelled the participants in the Human Potential Movement "soft revolutionaries." The new psycho-religiosity thus seen becomes an attack on the inability of many to participate meaningfully in the prevailing social structure. The fact that its strategies have been deployed in the hope of "humanizing" business, government bureaucracy, the family, and the schools confirms this view of it.

On the other hand, the new psycho-religiosity must remain ineffective, precisely because of its very "unworldliness." The individual must look for the significance of his life purely in the "magical, mystery tour" of his own mind. The popularity of Carlos Castaneda's books, with their Don Juan legend, advertises the appeal of this condition. It is fitting that Castaneda's stories are set in the wild and unnamed stretches of the Southwestern desert. There Castaneda as an apprentice to the Yaqui Indian sorcerer Don Juan learns how to rid himself of his conventional habits of perception and moral judgment. He enters into a "separate reality" where fact and fiction, the familiar and the fantastical, fuse together and constantly reconstitute themselves like beads of quicksilver on a glassy surface. Castaneda gradually loses not only his instinctive sense of time and place, but his ability to locate the center of his world. His "world" is the marvelous, waking dream that Don Juan has implanted in his head, a dream which sweeps him in sudden and random journeys from Los Angeles to Mexico City, from a clump of chapparal somewhere in the boundless wilderness to the road to the City of Ixtlan. Ixtlan, in the book *Journey to Ixtlan*, represents the mystical "home" to which all weary voyagers of the mind yearn to return. But Don Juan divulges to Castaneda at the close of the book that Don Juan can never go home again. He must remain a wayfarer on the road which leads not to his chosen destination but into the uncharted infinity of lift.

We are not, of course, countenancing as an alternative the "worldly" mission of religion, psychology, or other institutions that Cox used to talk so daringly about, i.e., the unsponsored commitment to action and the pursuit of "relevance." The new psycho-religiosity *is* relevant to the needs of people today who cry out for personal recognition and purpose. The error of the Human Potential Movement consists in its illusion that the true springs of personal meaning reside in the individual, not the culture or a larger religious and symbolic heritage. The new psycho-religiosity concentrates only on the psyche, and further disconnects and alienates the person from society by glorifying his narcissism -- his natural idea that he is the sole creator of meaning, the arbiter of his own values. The Human Potential Movement consistently perceives family and society as latent threats to autonomy, as "big boss methods to squash conflicts."[14] Granted, this view of institutions has some justifications in the bankruptcy and vacuity of social arrangements which have as their only *raison d'être* the maintenance of affluence. Yet without any apprecialbe respect for institutions, with their support of stability and growth, the reformation of society cannot come about. The Human Potential Movement urges us to live entirely in the "now," to indulge and contemplate simply the data of psychic experience as it flows past us. The "communities" which it contrives are communities of "experience" -- communities only in the sense that programmed rap sessions, or secular camp meetings in which people recount the ecstasies of their private "conversions," are communities. They are not authentic social or institutional bodies deriving their vitality from people working and living together in the face of the various contingencies of worldly existence.

The architects of encounter groups like to think of themselves as "subcultures" serving as the seeds from which new forms of culture will germinate. But the encounter groups, with their exclusive interest in the interior components of personality, cannot supply the bricks and mortar of culture. Meditation, self-inquiry, and interiority may provide the spiritual nucleus of an organic community, as was the case with the medieval monasteries, but they do not suffice for *community itself*. The Benedictine brotherhoods were not organized solely for the life of interiority. *Ora et labora* ("prayer and work") was their motto, specifying that their struggle for daily bread was as much an indispensible and of the community as the vision of God. When the monasteries grew too individualistic and inner-directed, they became corrupt and went to seed.

Finally, the quest of the new psycho-religiosity for ever alluring avenues to mind-expansion makes it chronically dependent on the conservation of privilege and wealth. It is a truism that significant benefits from the Human Potential Movement almost universally require high tuition and fees, and that its clients by and large tend to come from the more opulent segments of society. The privatism in the ethic of the affluent finds its way undoubtedly into the life-styles of the Human Potential Movement, thereby impairing the formation of firm communal links possible only if its members were interdependent

on each other in some palpable, economic fashion. Time and
time again sociologists have shown that what keeps communities
and families together is not the indolent freedom of self-
analysis and self-expression, but the *physical* necessity of
survival, translatable into a religious ethic of *duty* and
mutual accountability. The end of affluence may make encounter
groups superfluous as people learn better to know, relate to,
and sacrifice for each through the common limitations and
exigencies imposed upon them by economic hardship or by social
oppression.

In short, the significance of the person can ultimately be
discovered only when persons have reciprocal tasks and obligations incumbent upon them. It is through one's perception of
other people's everyday needs followed by one's lively, natural,
and moral response to them, not by absorption in one's own
private musings, that the meaning of one's own person-hood or
place in life comes clear. One comes to *be oneself* through
active love and service to other selves. The "encounter
culture," therefore, as Thomas Oden calls the new psycho-
religiosity, is not a solution but a symptom -- "a clue to a
deeper hunger and alienation in our society."[15] It serves
through manipulation of our subconscious desires, intuitions,
and dreams to cradle the instantaneous illusion of warmth,
involvement, and sharing when the tangible basis of human
solidarity is missing. Psycho-religiosity becomes the kind
of opiate wrongly imputed by Marx to all religion -- an occasion for anesthetizing the pain of life without eradicating
the true causes of that pain, for allowing people to feel "OK"
or "happy" when maybe they should do a little creative worrying
or feel some righteous anger. It becomes an opiate for the
affluent middle classes who cannot rid themselves of the rootlessness and loss of corporate values with which money and
excessive leisure has afflicted them.

Theology and the Search for a Center

The mystical, esthetic, and self-expressive bent of the new psycho-religiosity betrays not only the source of its own inadequacy for giving persons secure identities, but also the major infirmity of modern culture itself: the loss of a symbolic center of meaning and value.

In theology the controversy over the person's need for a single focus for knowledge and action has reflected the growing uncertainty about what it takes to be authentically human in a world plundered of its former coherence. Martin Marty, in his illuminating tableau of American religion in the 70's, has talked about the "task of centering" for the churches -- the necessity of their searching "for the core of Christian tradition and experience."[16] It is, of course, not just Christianity that needs so to be investigated; but it is also the entirety of modern culture. The breaking apart of Christian thinking in recent years has merely gone along with the general centrifugal tendencies in society. The burning question is whether to attempt to put Humpty-Dumpty back together again, or to try to find the hand of providence in the breakup.

Some years back the late Yale theologian and ethicist, H. Richard Niebuhr, grappled with this question in his *Radical Monotheism and Western Culture*. The traditon of religious monotheism, Niebuhr argued, does not betoken merely an intellectual assent to the unitary nature of God; it certifies a singular moral and cognitive foundation for society. The belief in one God for all the faithful is a single "center of value" holding together a culture. Polytheism appears in a culture in transition or in decay -- where the meaning of life as a whole is precarious, where people divide their loyalties among multiple causes or objectives which they worship as different gods and goddesses. The polytheistic notion that

"God" is not a unified personality, that divinity is distributed among a host of powers and spirits, some beneficent, some malign, some banal, arises with the dispersion of the center of value and the random acceptance of various and often conflicting moral standards or life goals. It amounts to the disappearance of an indivisible model of personhood and the absorption of the individual in romantic myths he may fashion for himself. Radical monotheism, therefore, constitutes an all-embracing scheme of meaning and motivation by which the riddles of existence can be deciphered and the ambiguities of decision-making in a complex world dispelled. Niebuhr writes that the "reference" of "radical monotheism" is "to no one reality among the many but to one beyond all the many, whence all the many derive their being, and by participation in which they exist. As faith, it is reliance on the source at all being for the significance of the self and of all that exists."[17]

Not surprisingly, Niebuhr's novel justification of monotheism has been assailed by David Miller, the theologian of play. Miller has moved from his earlier paean to the freedom of subconscious expression and fantasy to a theoretical defense of polytheism as a more viable symbolic universe for humanity in the contemporary age. His *The New Polytheism* offers a shrewdly reasoned apology for the homeless mind. Eschewing Niebuhr for Nietzsche, Miller comments that "the multiple patterns of polytheism allow room to move meaningfully through a pluralistic universe. They free one to affirm the radical plurality of the self, an affirmation that one has seldom been able to manage because of the guilt surrounding monotheism's insidious implication that we have to 'get it all together.'"[18] The new polytheism, Miller declares, makes much sense these days because of "the diversity of our new themes and their accompanying life-styles."[19] For "radical experience of the plurality of both social and psychological life" leads one to discover that "a single story, a monovalent logic, a rigid theology, and a confining morality are not adequate to help in understanding the nature of real meaning."[20]

Again we detect in Miller's language the breeze putdown of the integral life with such pejoratives as "rigid" and "confining." Miller seems to be upset about any God or culture that makes demands upon people, that calls them from the empty freedom of arbitrary choice and experiment, of narcissism and faddism, and confers on them new life with concrete purpose. "The nature of real meaning" is the absence of real meaning. Unlike the old polytheism of Graeco-Roman culture, which involved a certain civic responsibility and engagement in various aspects of normative culture, the new polytheism is, as Miller says, conductive to "anarchy." The "gods" of the new ploytheism are simply the myriad subconscious promptings and powers within the self. Like the new psycho-religiosity, the new polytheism tolerates them all and leaves the task of sorting them out in the hands of the individual alone.

Monotheism, of course, historically has not been as rigid as Miller thinks. The separation of sexuality and spirituality, mind and body, is the legacy of neo-Platonic dualism, which grew out of the confusion of polytheistic religion and culture. Biblical monotheism, agreeable with Niebuhr's paradigm, succeeds in reconciling the countless contingencies of human experience through the doctrine of the sovereign God, of humanity made in his image, and of the creation under his guidance which he has pronounced as "good." Monotheism delineates the center of value in which all values are ordered and illumined.

The new polytheism, however, asks that the "center" be located in each separate value itself, which suggest nothing more than extreme value-relativism, a studied *amorality*, as it were. Bona fide personhood is impossible within the new polytheism, for with it the content of personality is diffues; the principle which gets a person "together" has been ruled out of court.

The literary incarnation of Miller's new polytheistic adept is Henrik Ibsen's legendary playboy, Peer Gynt. In the play by the same name, Ibsen portrays a sophisticated, free-spirited man of the world who defies convention and tradition to flood his senses with the raw experience of living. Peer's motto is given to him by trolls: "To thine own self be enough." The lesson of Ibsen's play, though, is that one cannot so become a self or person. One's self is not enough. At the end of his life Peer is asked by the button-molder, who symbolizes the final assessment every individual makes about what he has done in his time, to define his own identity. Peer can point to the many thrills, conquest, and adventures he has undergone; he can say that he has tasted sweet and sour, exuberance and despair. He has, in a word, dabbled in all values, essayed many life styles, been enriched with wide experience of the world and the inner drama of the soul. Yet when it comes to finding his center, his real "self," Peer is discomfited. His self is like an onion: when all its layers are peeled away, it is nothing.

Affluence has created a society of onion-selves, or to employ T. S. Eliot's famous pharse, a society of "hollow men," men who have removed themselves from all tenancy in a world of interrelated meanings.

The pluralistic and Protean personality that Miller extols is a weak solution to the problem, the decline of affluence. Indeed, it slurs over the problem entirely. For the new polytheism must flag and flounder in an age when a lowered standard of living and pressing need for getting along on a day-to-day basis does not afford one the luxury of visiting all the exotic island of the psyche or surveying every *terra incognita* of the human spirit. The homeless mind is impelled to look for a home once more, not only because it can no longer navigate in the barrens of contemporary experience, but because the end of affluence hauls the giddy, soaring spirit of the new polytheist back to earth. It impels the homeless mind to look for a home once more. The gods of the new polytheism are slowly dying because the pressure of worldly events forces the denizens of today's world to seek an immobile center of meaning from which to deal concertedly with the crisis of survival. In other words, the summons is to recover a tradition.

NOTES TO CHAPTER 3

1. Marianne Gareheim, *Woodstock West: Five Days of Freedom* (Littleton: Matchless Publishing Co., 1970).

2. Erik Erikson, *Identity, Youth, and Crisis* (New York: Norton & Co., 1968), p. 81.

3. Peter Berger, *The Homeless Mind* (New York: Random House, 1973), p. 77.

4. Harvey Cox, *The Secular City* (New York: Macmillan, 1964), p. 47.

5. John Orr and Patrick Nichelson, *The Radical Suburb* (Philadelphia: Westminster Press, 1970).

6. John Locke, *Two Treatises of Government* (Cambridge: Cambridge University Press, 1963), p. 311.

7. Max Stirner, *The Ego and His Own* (London: Jonathan Cape, 1971), p. 99.

8. Alvin Toffler, *Future Shock* (New York: Random House, 1970), p. 87-88.

9. Alvin Toffler, *The Eco-Spasm Report* (New York: Books, 1975), p. 70.

10. cf. Muriel James, *Born to Love* (Redding: Addison - Wesley, 1973), also Muriel James and Dorothy Jongeward (Redding: Addison-Wesley, 1971).

11. William Schutz, *Joy* (New York: Grove Press, 1967), p. 5.

12. cf. Jerome Liss, *Free to Feel* (New York: Praeger, 1974), p. 3.

13. John E. Biersdorf, "The Human Potential Movement and the Church," *Christianity & Crisis* 35 (1975-1976), p. 56.

14. Liss, *op. cit.*, p. 4.

15. Thomas Oden, *Game Free* (New York: Harper & Row, 1974), p. 133.

16. Martin Marty, *The Fire We Can Light* (Garden City: Doubleday & Co., 1973), p. 219.

17. Richard Niebuhr, *Radical Monotheism and Western Culture* (New York: Harper & Row, 1960), p. 32.

18. David Miller, *The New Polytheism* (New York: Harper & Row, 1974), p. ix.

19. Miller, p. 2.

20. Miller, p. 11.

CHAPTER 4

The Recovery of Tradition

"What is past is prologue."

--Shakespeare, *The Tempest*

Tradition and Modernity

Sometime in the 1960's a whole generation forgot how to use the past tense. The nickname of "the now generation" was only a memorandum of the youthful disaffection with everything that had gone before. Popular pundits and academics lamented the growing ignorance of history. There was a well-circulated joke about the "latest" account of world history. The Creation, so the gag went, occurred in 1964 with the Free Speech protests in Berkeley, the Fall with the start of the Vietnam War in 1965, the Crucifixion with the assasination of Martin Luther King in 1968, and the Second Coming with the exoneration of the Chicago Seven. Interestingly, such humor had already done its rounds well before the re-election of Nixon in 1972 and the advent of the Watergate scandal.

It was, however, somewhat gratuitous to blame the young people of the 60's alone for having renounced history and tradition. Their preoccupation with the present moment, their flair for those colorful and meteoric media events called "happenings," were only mass expressions of the general loss of the sense of "pastness" that had been coming on over the years. The young emerged the old with their madcap innovations in dress, manners, and language, yet the old secretly sought to imitate them, largely because the vacuity of middle-class existence had left them with hardly any wisdom of their own to counter with. The "traditions" clung to by many graying Americans were husks of a once vital culture. Patriotism had declined into a mindless "follow-the-leader" mentality and a phobia about Communism, the work ethic into mere acquisitiveness, religion into golf-and-football Sundays. The "conservatism" espoused by the older generation proved itself to be nothing more than a feint for self-interest and cynicism. At least the young made no pretense about preserving what had already putrefied.

The impoverishment of the historical sense and the feeling for tradition has been a documented characteristic of the modern world. Social change, brought about by an ever rising and more complex standard of living, has made the trend inevitable. Traditions can be sustained only when there remains a coherent and ongoing basis of common experience, when people are constrained by some wider necessity to band together and to share the same assumptions about reality. These assumptions are held by young and old alike, their experiences not diverging much from each other. In a world where tradition is important, the form of culture is what Margaret Mead has termed "postfigurative:" the young time and time again are inducted into, or "configured" by, the massive body of "truths" and symbols passed on to them by their elders.

In the modern world, though, according to Mead, culture has turned "prefigurative." Tradition is lost and authority is inverted. Instead of the old catechizing the young, the young instruct the old, mainly because what is new or future seems to be more real and meaningful, and the later generations inevitably are one-step ahead of the times. Fresh "experiences" of a world forever in flux are the province of the young, with whom the old are incessantly trying to play "catch-up." Parents coyly copy their children's clothing or experiment with marijuana; ministers and teachers are urged to "get with it" by catering to the tastes and expectations of their charges. *Tradition*, which in the original Latin meant a "handing down" of lore from generation to generation, becomes *tradition* -- the endless passage of attention from novelty to novelty, from one sensation to the next.

The waning of tradition in modern society has for a long time been considered an irreversible if not an unhealthy development. In much sociological literature of the past few decades the word "modernization" as a matter of course has been contrasted with "traditionalism." Indeed, the word "tradition" has gradually taken on pejorative connotations. It has come to imply rigidity, insensitivity, and downright superstition, not to mention stifling conformism, anti-democratic government, and the suppression of rights of minorities and women. More and more we tend to picture "traditionsl" societies as backward and benighted, infected with prejudice and chauvinism. Among intellectuals tradition means preserving the ways of the past for their own sake, like making the sign of the cross or saying the pledge of allegiance before sports events simply because that is what people have always done. As a contemporary British writer has caustically phrased the issue: "I find myself getting haunted by the thought that we're approaching a breakthrough where everything we do or say will relate back to something done or said in the past, and we shall have become not so much a notion as a breathing archive."[2] The modern intellectual gripes that his creativity, his self-image or uniqueness, is hamstrung by outworn rules, procedures, and fashions. Yet he is not reacting to tradition itself so much as to the *absence of tradition*. When vital traditions disintegrate, the result is often an attempt by those in power to require allegiance to alien ideas or to enforce empty customs and unjust laws. The appeal to dead traditions leads to a cult of *traditionalism*. Today it is the problem of traditionalism, not tradition *per se*, which is the source of much confusion.

The eminent political scientist, Carl Friedrich, has characterized traditionalism as an "ideology" which is "a self-conscious and deliberate insistence upon the value of tradition, making it a norm of behavior...elaborated into an action program," a program which frequently becomes "reactionary."[3] Tradition, on the other hand, is no such ideology or program. Rather, it is "a set of established values and beliefs having persisted over several generations."[4] In other words, traditions sprout, blossom, and decay in the soil of lived experience -- they represent consistent ways of grappling with and interpreting that experience so that the path of social evolution can be steadied. Traditionalism, on the other hand, is the employment of makeshift concepts to nurse the illusion of tradition. Social scientists tell us that traditionalism gains sway in periods of rapid modernization and upheaval when individuals or groups reach out for some dogma that will make contemporary experience seem less chaotic. The political fundamentalism of the John Birch Society and the revival of old tribal ways in many emerging nations exemplify the self-conscious and *ad hoc* strategies of the traditionalists. Genuine traditions, however, neither have to be encouraged through propaganda nor imposed by government decree. They "come natural" inasmuch as people assume their viability, and find the view of the world and moral codes which they enshrine to be eminently suitable to their everyday aspirations and self-understanding. It is virtually a contradiction in terms to brand a tradition "irrelevant" to the times, since the relevancy of tradition is what makes it worthy of respect among members of a society, and of transmission to posterity.

The so-called lack of "flexibility" in traditions, therefore, is owed mainly to the false conformity and security sought by traditionalists. What modern intellectuals have perceived as a monolithic authoritarianism and lack of spontaneity in traditional cultures has been shown recently to be a misapprehension. D. N. Levine notes that the hallmarks of traditional societies is not gray uniformity and censorship of individual expression. Those are features of totalitarian societies, which attempt to carve traditions out of nothing. Rather, traditional societies are characterized by their sense of "solidarity" grounded in a true feeling of historical community and shared purpose.[5] One can think of Elizabethan England, for instance, as an instance of "traditional culture," yet it hardly compares with the "blue ant" society of today's China. It has been the demise of living traditions, together with the rise of normless individualism, which has led inevitably to social repression and lock-step conformity. The Frenchman Alexis De Tocqueville noted over a century ago how, for example, the American obsession with individuality went hand in glove with a fear of real deviation from average behavior. It has been said that true eccentrics have been more readily tolerated in countries with traditional social structures, like France or Britain, than in this country, where loyalty oaths in employment and the bland insistence that everyone be "100 percent American" have proven powerful checks against dissidence. Traditional cultures spin a web within which variable expressions of personality are possible. Traditionless cultures leave it all up to the individual yet out of fear of chaos or anarchy ultimately leave little room for creative innovation. The upshot is a thin-skinned traditionalism based on nostalgic dreams rather than on the maintenance of authentic values.

Affluence, Conservatism, and Totalitarianism

Anxiety about undirected change in a traditionless society generates a variety of pseudo-traditions, just as the ethic of individual autonomy conduces to the creation of pseudo-identities. Unfortunately, in the United States such pseudo-traditions have centered mainly on the comfortable morality which undergirds affluence and uncritical dedication to material gain. In the so-called "conservative" mind, the "tradition" of political freedom involves the defense of predatory capitalism and the irresponsible acquisition of wealth. Religious fundamentalism has just as often been tied to a principled defense of cherished spiritual values and beliefs as a means of keeping an easy conscience in the face of prophetic criticism about the church's sanctioning of the economic status quo. Outside the South, fundamentalist churches tend to be the richest ones. The great pseudo-tradition which has fatefully inspired Americans in the twentieth century has been that of the "good life" for whoever finds it.

But the aim of the good life in an economy of abundance has actually been the destruction of traditions. The consumer ethic and the passion for making a buck has contributed to the break-up of traditional communal associations, particularly the family, their life becoming subordinate to the quickening of economic output.[6] Pastors annually rue the commercialization of Christmas and Easter, yet few seriously call to task the entire system for making profit more important than ceremonial observances. And most holidays, originally occasions for extended family gatherings or neighborhood get-togethers, are now memorable solely for the number of highway deaths or the price and availability of gasoline for automobile trips.

Even capitalism itself, which according to famous economic historian Joseph Schumpeter once was tied up with the tradition of family loyalty and rule within a community (hence the legends of the great entrepreneurial families like the Vanderbilts and the Rockefellers), has been uprooted from its own social and moral heritage and assimilated to the bloodless and purely economic ends of corporate profit, productivity, and the yearly GNP. "Free enterprise" is not a tradition in itself. It is an economic myth which disguises the concentration of the means of production among conglomerates and federally supported cartels, such as the oil industry. The legacy of capitalism on Adam Smith's model of stalwart merchants and small property owners has slowly been transformed into the impersonal process of affluence operating within a moral and cultural void. Government economists, for instance, seldom talk about the problems of the nation in terms of the work ethic, ownership of property, or the tangible sufferings and disruption of family life caused by unemployment; mainly they discuss, abstractly and with global reference, industrial output, capital formation, and extraction of natural resources. The human agents of the productive process are factored out by economic calculations. Similarly, the "impact statements" attached to recent government and industrial decisions rarely touch on the consequences of those decisions for families, towns, and education; they are concerned mainly with maintaining markets and with providing "incentives" for increasing the quantity of energy, goods, and services. The same thing is true in other industrialized countries, whether they call themselves capitalist or socialist.

The social effects of affluence, therefore, weaken the pillars of traditional culture at all levels. They do so mainly by divorcing the systematic objectives of enlarging aggregate wealth from the more humane goals of preserving cultural and interpersonal bonds among people and groups. Individualism replaces traditionalism, not because the iron hand of the past has been lifted in a creative burst of free thinking and expression, but because the individual has been abstracted from communal existence by the demands of employment in the productive process. Historically, the ideology of raw individualism has not been strongest in agrarian communities, small trading towns, or ethnic neighborhoods. It has been strongest in industrialized megalopolises where primary social groups are weak or absent and the pursuit of private well-being dwarfs other responsibilities. The "parochial" horizons of traditional communities, however, tend to leave the organization of work and the distribution of economic benefits as parts of a larger network of mutual co-operation and service. Maximum production is considered a good only if it causes no injury to the network of customary moral and social relationships forming the community. The result, as Edward Schumacher, a defender of traditional society and its scaled-down economic operations, has indicated, is actually a more desirable mode of living; excessive material wants and the lust for advantage are lacking.[7]

For over two centuries now the stability and connectedness of traditional society has been attacked by liberals for its fostering of economic inefficiency and stagnation. On the other hand, liberals have claimed that liberation of the individual from ancestral ties and loyalties has aided in the democratization of social and political life. Such an attitude inherently identifies traditional society with the political absolutism of the feudal society preceding the industrial revolution. The economic stagnation castigated by Adam Smith resulted less from the preservation of traditional values in European cultures than from the control of the national economies by the crown for the purpose of providing luxuries. The fault was political rather than social or cultural. Even today it has been the curb on democratic participation in many

Third world countries that has supported an imbalance of wealth between the very rich and the very poor, as well as inhibited improvement of the overall standard of living. So it has been, for example, with Brazil. Their assault on traditional ways by alliance of the military with multinational corporations has hiked the annual output of that nation's economy while accentuating general poverty and creating a police state. In the United States, dissolution of rural communities through the abandonment of small family farms, and the blight of urban middle class neighborhoods where local businesses were once numerous, has meant the decline of traditional group associations and greater social mobility and economic opportunity. More significantly, it has made people lose the reins of their own destinies while sacrificing them to the power of the large corporations -- hardly an enhancement of "democracy" in the true sense of the word.

Traditional culture in the past, sustained by grassroots associations and popular institutions, has actually been a bulwark against exploitation, while bureaucratic and totalitarian management has thrived on the formation of masses of rootless individuals. The sociologist, Robert Nisbet observes that the real struggle for freedom in Western history has not been between the state and the individual, but between the state and smaller, communal organizations such as churches, fraternities, guilds, and labor unions.[8] The state, in its modern form, has grown up on the rubble of native values and institutions. The push for state control has largely accompanied the increase in complexity and specialization of the national economy. A sophisticated and highly integrated national economy requires central authority and a more streamlined apparatus for decision-making, and it has been only natural that smaller, traditional units of power and authority have abdicated their functions. Whether the broadening of state control has been direct, as in the case of "socialist" governments, or indirect, as in federal support of monopolies and trusts, the result has been the promotion of prosperity at the expense of fragile cultural links between people. Again it has not been so much the numerous strides in technology that have encouraged state supervision of daily affairs (the use of fast transportation, mass communications, data banks, etc.), though these have been important factors; rather it has been the need for more efficient operation of the production process. Where human wants are minimal and the means for satisfying them straightforward, the power of the state is not complete, save in the event of military conquest. Today's totalitarian regimes have sprung up when the mechanisms of production in modern society failed to supply a decent livelihood for the many. In many instances it has been the disappearance of alternative in a culture of affluence that seems to have made totalitarianism inevitable.[9]

Regardless of whether the state intervenes in a totalitarian or in a more benign manner, the extent of its role will be proportional to the absence or ineffectiveness of traditional associations in providing for the welfare of human beings. When a social order that was once a tough lattice of associations and institutions with their respective rights and responsibilities, both to their own members and to those of other groups, disintegrates into bare constituent elements, then the state is the only viable authority remaining to preserve harmony. When traditional society has been torn apart by the forces of centralized production aimed at increasing affluence, then the coming of a massive economic crisis, such as the one now in the offing, heightens the risk that the state will move in to supply communal bonds. The danger of totalitarianism thereby looms because of insufficient community resources to cope with the new situation.

Totalitarianism can easily masquerade as a new traditionalism which "solves" the problems of a fractured culture. The common-sense notion that the collapse of social order and economic transactions has something to do with the loss of a national purpose or a failure of the corporate "will" supports the ideology of totalitarians who, like Hitler, want to revive the solidarity of the *Volk* ("people"), or who, like the Communists, want to create a proletarian "consciousness" in all workers. The signature of totalitarianism is its passion to create overnight, through the dismantling of former life-styles and through intense propaganda, a new culture where traditional meanings and bonds are either soft or lacking. The customary authority embodied in historical and organic fellowships is supplanted by the educational and moral regimentation effected by state or "party." Traditional constraint vanishes before political terror. The interpersonal loyalties that are the substance of small-group life are played upon and manipulated in the cult of the "leader," who may be a surrogate father-figure or mother-figure. The pseudo-traditions of totalitarianism are usually justified as necessary correctives to the dissipation of established values by liberal politics. Thus, the Italian fascist, Mario Palmieri, in 1936 applauded the social arrangements of Mussolini as "a higher and more powerful expression of personality." The fascist state, he wrote,

> ...sums up all the manifestations of the moral and intellectual life of man. Its functions cannot therefore be limited to those of enforcing order and keeping the peace, as the liberal doctrine had it... the Fascist state is an inwardly accepted standard and rule of conduct, a discipline of the whole person; it permeates the will no less than the intellect. It stands for a principle which becomes the central motive of man as a member of civilized society, sinking deep down into his personality; it dwells in the heart of the man of action and of the thinker,

>of the artist and of the man of science: soul of
>the soul. Fascism, in short, is not only a law-
>giver and a founder of institutions, but an
>educator and promoter of spiritual life. It aims
>at refashioning not only the forms of life but their
>content -- man, his character and his faith. To
>achieve this purpose it enforces discipline and uses
>authority, entering into the soul and ruling with
>undisputed sway.[10]

In short, the totalitarian idea of the state entails the internalization of prescribed ethics and attitudes as the basis of a larger tradition. The only difference between the method of the totalitarians and the authority of traditional culture is that whereas the latter evolves out of the historical experience of a people, the former is systematically and rigorously executed as the utopian vision of a self-appointed elite. Totalitarian manipulation of people's feelings and thoughts becomes possible, however, only when the traditional media of meaning and identity no longer operate.

The Need for New Traditions

We thus come to a consideration of the most pressing challenge of Western society in the twilight of affluence: the need for new traditions. Without the mastic of tradition, the economic chaos that may conceivably beset Western society in the near future could end in some form of despotism. For tyrannical regimes promise not only bread, but also a new order of life in which the earning of one's portion can be sanctified in terms of some mighty cause. Affluence, as social critics left and right have tirelessly remarked, dulls people's sensibilities to meaningful human contacts, dries up the hallowed sources of meaning and value, becomes the end-all and be-all of existence. In reaction the search for a secure frame of orientation turns desperate and invites the pedaling by political wizards of what Eric Voegelin has termed "the magic of the extreme." It is no accident that the abject economic conditions in Germany in the 1920's and 30's, which followed in the wake of the dissolution of the nation's old social and cultural order after World War I, inspired in most Germans a yearning for some superhuman Messiah who would set their world aright again. Political saviors who exploit economic deprivation and social discontent with vague pledges about recapturing old virtues and manners are not that uncommon even in America nowadays, as the George Wallace phenomenon among the lower middle classes recently evidenced.

The historical irony is that traditions cannot be conjured up in political platforms or by government edicts. Traditionalism as an express political policy must either falter altogether or turn into fascism. Authentic traditions, unlike their mere semblance, must be nurtured within institutions and communities as the mature fruits of work and collaboration. Although the dead past cannot be completely resurrected, communities can harken to the wisdom of the past in order to reinterpret and refashion it for the exigencies of the moment. It is true, as Dryden intoned, that "not Heav'n itself upon the past has pow'r," yet the past does have the power to compel a new assessment of what is both possible and provident for the future. New traditions must enter the cultural mainstream, carrying with them the sediment of what was meaningful to generations past. In the new traditional society the experiences of the present are not carelessly squeezed into rigid, old molds, but are modified by the mature perspectives of all generations. Such, in religion, was the story of Reformation Europe some five hundred years ago.

The fountain head of any new tradition, however, must lie within history itself. It must not be the history popularly venerated like that of the bleached bones of martyrs and saints, nor the history reconstructed in finicky detail by antiquarian scholars, but the history come alive in the ongoing experiences of a community of faith. The form of the historical experience that animates a tradition is an experience which gives history itself significance and purpose. H. Richard Niebuhr has described such an experience as "revelation," or "history as it is lived and apprehended from within."[11] Revelation furnishes the inner meaning of history, the compass and ballast of human existence throughout time. Revelation locates a community within history and clarifies its purpose within the sweep of events. The "authority" of the past regarded in terms of revelation, therefore, does not lock a community into the rote worship of ancient images, but serves as a map of all history by which human beings can guide their current and future lives. Revelation is, in fact, what makes history and establishes tradition; it is what discloses the psychological and social relevance of corporate symbols and cloaks them with contemporary import. The past then becomes not a conclusion to the drama of humanity but a prologue to an epic yet to be fully narrated.

Finally, revelation establishes the bounds of humanity's historical freedom and allays the terror of decision in both the long and short run. Revelation is the final adjudicator of human values. The homeless mind of modernity, intoxicated with the heady wine of affluence, power, and galloping change, has latched on to the false notion that every individual can peg together his own symbols and value system with the alacrity and caprice of a child working on an erector set. Yet, as C. S. Lewis has gamely commented: "The human mind has no more power of inventing a new value than of imagining a new primary colour, or, indeed, of creating a new sun and a new sky for it to move in."[12] Values are not arbitrary constructs but the biological and cognitive keys to the endurance of societies and of the race. Revelation is the moment of divine insight or inspiration wherein the key becomes apparent. Traditions tend to conform themselves to the shape of this inspiration, to codify and make plain what has emerged in a flash of intuition to seers or prophets. The pseudo-traditions of the totalitarians and the social engineers turn out to be invidious, since they seek to secure a basis for human life which does not well up from the depth of group wisdom and practice. Theirs are ideologies rather than the richer resonances of lived experience.

Moreover, ideologies derive from the illusion that human beings can freely decide, according to faddish, intellectually appealing schemes, what ought to be thought or accomplished. A tradition, on the other hand, is dictated by unconscious, not manifestly theoretical considerations. Traditions have as their sole rationale the transcendence of private ambitions or individual preferences by the crystallizing of a moral unity for human endeavor. Traditions are not consciously designed by human beings; they grow organically out of their reciprocal needs. In this respect traditions conflict with the modern categorical imperative of absolute freedom. They do not sanction individual liberty in the extreme so much as give new significance and worth to historical necessity. In Shakespeare's words, they

> Teach thy necessity to reason thus;
> There is no virtue like necessity.

The "virtue of necessity" turns on its head the abstract model of freedom present in contemporary liberal culture, the "freedom" of privatism and insular individualism. For example, in the Christian tradition freedom incorporates freedom to do the will of God, and in the humanism of the classical West freedom included freedom to do the good. Yet the good is inalterably defined by wider parameters than mere individual choice. In the era of the end of affluence, the "good" must be installed as the kind of virtue which binds together the broken symbols of the past with the discontinuous worlds of individuals who have no sense of a common life to which they could belong.

The need for a new tradition, or traditions, issues therefore from the necessity of physical survival, if not of that alone. Robert Heilbroner in his *An Inquiry into the Human Prospect* speculates that the society of the future will

> ...turn in the direction of many pre-industrial societies -- toward the exploration of inner states of experience rather than the outer world of fact and material accomplishment. Tradition and ritual, the pillars of life in virtually all societies other than those of an industrial character, would probably once again assert their ancient claims as the guide and solace for life. The struggle for individual achievement, especially for material ends, is likely to give way to the acceptance of communally organized and ordained roles.[13]

Material abundance and the gearing of national industry to "individual achievement, especially for material ends," has both demanded and made possible the "liberation" of the individual from traditional ways and thinking. That both a subsistence standard of living and the "good life" could be smugly taken for granted has led to a slackening of community and family links which remain strong when people contended together against adversity. Children need not feel sure ties with their parents because of the social freedom provided by easy money. The same is true with spouses; both can draw handsome salaries while pursuing their own lives. The mutual aid networks running through old ethnic neighborhoods became superfluous when their people grew so well-fixed that they could be independent of each other and move to the suburbs. Even the joint ownership of consumer durables and sharing of services, as in local "co-ops," seems little more than a quaint

habit when everyone can afford his own luxuries. Economic
scarcity, however, brings into relief the fact of human
interdependence -- witness the switch from single driver
commuting to car pools under the duress of gasoline shortages
in 1974. On the basis of this human interdependence vital
traditions can emerge.

Traditions, though, rest on symbolic and emotional
attachments among people more than on alliances of convenience.
The end of affluence may finally engrave on the public consciousness the recognition that deep and long-term commitments
among people are not just practical considerations for making
life easier; they are what humanize us, giving us a true sense
of place in the panorama of birth, life, and death. The now
nostalgic model of the farm family and the agricultural village
in which people consecrate their lives together in tilling the
soil and sharing the bane and blessings of a common destiny may
ultimately have import for a new urban civilization where loneliness, alienation, and anomie could be overcome through a
central experience of real fellowship.[14] For the virtue of
necessity can be turned into a joyful and hopeful affirmation
of a common set of tasks galvanized through the revelation of
a higher purpose. Though prophecy is risky and perhaps presumptuous, we can sketch some of the new forms of culture that
may prove to be the cores of new traditions.

The Cores of Tradition: Communes, Co-operatives or Neighborhoods?

The core of any tradition, as we have suggested, is the
strength and solidity of the social groups who are its custodians and who maintain it among themselves and over the
generations. The revival of tradition, therefore, depends
on such groups. Certainly their formation is not just a
pious wish. The ethic of "coming together" prevalent in
the 60's spawned various voluntary associations, most

notably the commune, over-against the conspicuous lack of bona fide communities in the affluent society. In 1972 Keith Melville observed that the "lexicon of the communal movement reflects a conscious desire to return to the integral community of preindustrial society."[15] Communes describing themselves as "families" or "tribes" hint of this longing.

The communal movement of the 1960's and early 70's, however, was largely confined to the vanguard of the counter-culture, and suffered from several defects. In the first place, many of the communes had no coherent body of values around which to organize. As Ron Roberts, another student of contemporary communes points out, much of the counter-cultural homesteading in California and New Mexico was undertaken mainly as a haven for drug-users and those who did not want to be "hassled" by societal pressures. Such "communities" never got off the ground, and many folded almost immediately, partly because of their rejection of group discipline, partly because their members wanted to do little more than get high, make love, and lie about in insouciant indolence.[16] The "do-your-own-thing" morality proved inimicable to lasting communality. Other communes incorporated with a distinct aim and method of social control, for example Twin Oaks in Virginia, have fared better, as Katherine Kinkade in her vivid account of the group's struggle for success relates.[17] On the other hand, many communes have suffered from their inexperience in the farming or the running of light industry, such as handicrafts, necessary for their well-being. While they have sought to be self-sufficient, the maintenance of even their modest life-style has been dependent on an inflow of money from the larger society. Thus the Lama Foundation in New Mexico, a fairly prosperous multi-religious commune founded during the past decade, draws a good deal of its income not from internal sources but from the private holdings of new members, from the sale of books and pamphlets, and from fees levied on overnight visitors. In short, the preservation of the communities cannot be separated from the availability of excess wealth on the outside.

In the second place, many communes have not provided a traditional framework through which loyalty to the community enterprise can be perpetuated. The rapid turnover in membership implies that such communes are mainly "half-way houses" for alienated youths who sign up for a season in search of social therapy, then drift back into more conventional relationships. Those communes which seem to have staying power are run by religious sectarians, such as the Hutterites and the Bruderhof.[18] They are fortified with a tradition and a history, yet their very sectarian character prevents them from becoming models for the renewing of the greater culture. Their religious exclusivism and detachment from the world leave them immune to disruptive influences, but at the same time make them little more than museum exhibits. Contemporary communes, like religious sects as a whole, are valuable reminders of what life can be; they are provocative experiments in the refinement of human relations. Still, they do not offer types for reconstruction of the wider society and culture, unless we are talking about future social need amidst some kind of return to universal barbarism and anarchy, as in the Dark Ages when the medieval monasteries became the only exemplars of community. Despite the many Cassandras of the present age, that sort of social break-up is not likely to recur. The more sinister peril is the absorption of integral group life by the totalitarian state.

The local co-operative, as a second model, cannot be considered a community in the strict sense of the word. However, it may draw the community spirit upwards. Sociological studies have repeatedly shown that it is people *doing things together* -- things that affect them directly -- that makes for healthy community. When the tasks of the co-operative have to do with concerns and issues of deepest practical consequence, the incentive for creating and preserving community remains strong. In addition, co-operatives are nuclei around which the interests and needs of people in a given situation can gather. Requiring no withdrawal from work in the present society and from existing family arrangements, they operate against the isolation of people in today's urban setting. They enlarge daily contacts, open up communication, and help to extend the range of concern and service among individuals beyond the highly selective pairings of personal friendships. But co-operatives are only as good as the services they perform; all other benefits are incidental.

Co-operatives perhaps represent the type of economic bonding that will have to take place in the post-affluent society, but they do not provide the ultimate satisfaction of intimate involvement and shared meaning. Many have become so huge that their members regard them as little more than public services, like inexpensive health clinics or garbage collection. One of the main problems with co-operatives instituted within the counterculture is the life-style of the individuals who belong to them. Many such co-operatives are composed of single, transient, and introverted young who see them as nothing more than temporary ways to "get involved" in something while they are in residence in school or passing through the city. Despite the appeals of these "common markets" to their members to take them as "their co-ops," to attend their business meetings, and to arrange social gatherings, the rootlessness of the young people composing them results in just about all the enthusiasm for them coming from their elected officers and their supervisory personnel. Cheap food is still the best bait.

Effective co-operatives are built on stable and unified neighborhoods. The age of affluence has witnessed the dismantling of neighborhood culture, both in the rooting of inner-city ethnic wards and the self-indulgent anonymity of suburbia. Neighborhood culture once embraced the private and public affairs of residents, not merely because everybody knew nearly everybody else, but also because such a culture was maintained through the proximity of work, recreation, and places of religious worship. Neighborhood culture was "street culture" and "pub cultures," or, for the younger set, "ice cream parlor culture," instead of living room culture, as is still in evidence from the multitudes of all ages who assemble in the evening on porches, on the corners of boulevards and in the honky-tonk taverns of say, Somerville, Massachusetts, or South Philadelphia. The absence of any strict demarcation between what goes on in the home and on the block at any given hour of the day suggests a throbbing nervous system of community life, even with a rising fear of crime in the cities and simmering racial tensions. James V. Cunningham, in an analysis of what forces build a vital neighborhoods, specifies a community newspaper or news organ to facilitate discussion of local issues, political and civic groups for dealing at the grassroots level with community problems, and families with leadership responsibility who have a sense of commitment to to the locale.[19] Donald and Rachell Warren have described the "integral neighborhood" as the cornerstone for the survival of democracy,[20] and have identified a number of factors which support it: regular interaction among citizens, a sense of neighborhood identity, mutual assistance, mobilization against bureaucratic manipulation from the outside, and connections with agencies outside the community. Interestingly, the Warrens have shown that the creation of such a neighborhood does not depend on a return to ethnic homogeneity or the leveling of social classes so much as on the marshaling of common sentiments among the local populace, which may be accomplished for various reasons. Furthermore, such a neighborhood is knit together by information channels that constantly reinforce the feeling of shared goals and mutual understanding of what is going on.

The Warrens do not talk about "tradition" as a feature of the integral neighborhood. The integral neighborhood, however, is latent in the social conditions that will arrive with the end of affluence. The loss of purchasing power for general luxuries will probably dampen the habit of using recreation as an "escape" from the environment in which individuals spend much of their time. Instead of ski weekends and drives in the country, gatherings in yards and parks may become the new pastime and not need to be a mainstay of the "old" ways. The integral neighborhood thus can be formed out of a variety of human materials already present. The crucial ingredient is a consensus that personal needs relate somehow at many levels, from the need for street improvements to the need for artistic activities. Out of such a rudimentary consensus the awareness of related experiences and challenges can be derived.

On the other hand, a neighborhood can never achieve importance in people's lives so long as they view it as marginal to what really matters. "Welcome wagons" and neighborhood improvement associations are found even in the suburbs, but they are inadequate for generating community spirit so long as people's careers and private interests have overwhelming priority. The end of affluence, entailing the drying up of high-pressure and high-paying jobs for the many, may lead to a "waste" of education and talent, but it may also cause a curtailment of careerism and thus encourage people to relocate the centers of their lives in their immediate surroundings. Such prospects are perhaps abhorrent to those who have prized personal mobility and "self-achievement" as unquestioned goods, yet a forced retreat from the values of privatism may in the long run have salutary consequences. It may give a new content to our experiences that we have never learned to appreciate.

The Church

We would pursue a tedious theme here to discuss how or who the church has become for many a feeble institution which over the years has lost much of its social prestige and significance. Vital and active churches still abound throughout the country, but there is little doubt, as Gallup polls attest, that church-going and engagement in total church life has been on the wane since the 1950's. The "irrelevance" of the establishment churches has been a pet topic among liberal clergy. And there is reasonable justification for many of the complaints. The American churches, especially in the twentieth century, have merely mirrored the decadent morality of affluence in many ways: the emphasis on private piety to the detriment of community outreach, the tepid concern for hard moral and social issues, the love affair with church buildings (the so-called "edifice complex") as garish emblems of privilege and wealth, not to mention the assimilation of Christianity to the "American way of life." Church policy and organization have more and more followed the lead of the business corporation, as sociologist Peter Berger has convincingly argued, in the growth of unwieldy bureaucracies tooled up to package and "sell" a particular religious "product."[21] In protest against this contemporary "Babylonian captivity" of the church, new and radical models of ecclesiastical participation have been proposed, including different versions of the "underground church," the "people's church," or churches led by "tentmaking" ministers (after the fashion of the early church which had no salaried staff but was led by ministers self-supported through working at secular jobs, as did Paul, who made tents). Unfortunately, a reform-minded clergy and parishioners have chronically fallen to faddism and to the identification of the church with whatever ephemeral cult of sensibility happens along. So many of these "experimental" churches have gone the way of the Sexual Freedom League and Haight-Ashbury.

Yet the recovery of tradition cannot be separated from a renaissance of the church as a leading institution in modern culture. This is because the churches have historically been the repositories of tradition. Not only did they preside over the intellectual and social life of people in cities and towns; they also were community centers. We were all taught in grade school how in early America the church was the ganglion of personal relationships and cultural activities: a forum for debating local and national issues, a recreation hall, a shelter and welfare agency for the indigent.

The disappearance of the church from the center stage of life has paralleled the shrinking and compartmentalizing of religion as a subjective or "Sabbath" phenomenon. Secularism has taken its toll. On the other hand, the churches have also been a powerful antibody against the more pernicious diseases of secularism. Leonard Schapiro and others have cited the churches as the prime movers in the resistance to fascism during the 1930's and 40's.[22] Later, in the Vietnam period, despite their congregations clergymen of all denominations were the most vocal "establishment" group in opposition to the outrages of American war policy. They had a far better record on the main than businessmen, Congressmen, and perhaps even university administrators.

Yet the distinguishing mark of the church has been its unmatched role as the formulator and guardian of religious symbols which reflect the "ultimate concerns" of a people. Tradition requires a feeling of permanent place, not only in the geographic sense, but also in a cosmic mode. Thus religious institutions cannot be omitted from any discussion of the resurgence of traditional life. In the words of Nisbet:

> The reason why religion has figured so prominently in social history is that in any community a feeling of meaning, of shared purpose, is essential to the prosperity of the community. Religion, traditionally, has been the vessel in which most of the shared meanings and purposes of a deeper sort have been carried.[23]

In the Middle Ages the order of religious meanings was intertwined with the order of society. The parish church, as a locus of community life, was regarded in the popular imagination and in theological doctrine as one rung in an ascending ladder of value and authority which encompassed both "Christendom" -- the rather vague idea of European culture united in a single faith -- and the metaphysical hierarchy of angels, heavens, and God himself. In the modern world the development of religious and political pluralism dissolved the integral myth of the Middle Ages, and traditions were confined to particular national, social, and ethnic connumities. Churches came to express and validate the meaning systems of those communities within the framework of more ancient Christian symbols. Under the impact of the affluent society, the frittering away of communities carried the process one step further; and such a development has been perhaps as important a factor as science and technology in the decline of the churches. When all coherent meaning systems are reduced to radically individual and subjective worlds of experience the influence of every institution, including the church, goes by the board.

Hardly anyone would suggest that the recovery of tradition means a return to the integral culture of the Middle Ages, or even the restoration of the old national and ethnic communities. Traditionalists who yearn to turn the clock back will be as disappointed as those who glory uncritically in the new and

untried. The churches in many ways have already abdicated
their historical responsibility to mediate genuine traditional
ideas and values, largely because the cultural equipment for
the transmission of those ideas and values has gone to ruin.
The much heralded recent spurt in membership within the
so-called "conservative" churches, as described in Dean Kelly's
Why Conservative Churches are Growing,[24] does not necessarily
point to a rebirth of genuine Christianity. Kelly rightly
commends the "conservative" churches for inspiring involvement
and commitment to one's faith in contrast to the mainline,
liberal denominations, who have drifted with the diffuse social
movements of the past decade. It is difficult to conclude,
however, that many of the conservative churches are doing more
than providing another spiritual sop for those who cling to
the privatized life-styles of affluence. The type of conservative churches that seem to be increasingly "successful" are
still largely the citadels of wealth, privilege, and right-wing
politics.

The pseudo-conservatism of the Nixon years, which such a
trend reflects, is vastly different from the renascent traditional culture that lies close to the historical horizon. The
traditions of that culture will break forth out of new social
and economic circumstances betokening a yet unconceived religious situation. Likewise, the rededication of the churches
to the life of solidarity in times of economic scarcity will
serve to reinvest and embody the meaning of the new traditions.
The actual form of the "new" traditional church is open to
conjecture. It may be, as the pundits say, that the days of
"organized religion as we have known it for all these years
are numbered." Yet religion must remain "organized" in some
sense so long as human culture itself retains a structure. A
"disorganized" religion is what we have too much of nowadays,
just as we are suffering from the nihilism and anomie of a

society teetering on its own shoddy undergirdings. The *re-organization* of religion will come about with the rehabilitation of the common life. And the place to begin is the very ganglion of such life -- the family.

NOTES TO CHAPTER 4

1. For this distinction see Margaret Mead, "The Future: Prefigurative Cultures and Unknown Children," in Alvin Toffler (ed.), *The Futurists* (New York: Random House, 1972), pp. 27-50.

2. M. Shrapnel, "To Hell with Tradition," *New Statesman* (Feb. 4, 1966), p 157.

3. Carl Friedrich, *Tradition and Authority* (New York: Praeger, 1972), pp. 18-19.

4. Friedrich, p. 18.

5. cf. D. N. Levine, "Flexibility and Traditional Culture," *Journal of Social Issues* (Oct. 1968).

6. cf. J. Hitchcock, "The Use of Tradition," *Review of Politics* (Jan. 1973).

7. cf. E. F. Schumacher, *Small is Beautiful* (New York: Harper & Row, 1973).

8. Robert Nisbet, *The Quest for Community* (Oxford: Oxford University Press, 1953), p 106f.

9. William Ebenstein, for example, argues that the lure of totalitarian regimes in times of economic crisis is their ability to stimulate growth and to enforce saving or spending when the natural or social processes for accomplishing the same ends are weak. cf. *Totalitarianism: New Perspectives* (New York: Holt, Rinehart & Winston, 1962), p. 61.

10. Mario Palmieri, *The Philosophy of Fascism* (Chicago: Dante Alighieri Society, 1936), p. 131.

11. H. Richard Niebuhr, *The Meaning of Revelation* (New York: Macmillan, 1941), p. 60.

12. C. S. Lewis, *The Abolition of Man* (New York: Macmillan, 1947), pp. 56-70.

13. Robert Heilbroner, *An Inquiry into the Human Prospect* (New York: W. W. Norton, 1974), p 146.

14. The experience of communion in an agricultural setting is described vividly by Benjamin Zablocki in his study of the Bruderhof community. cf. *The Joyful Community* (Baltimore: Penguin Books, 1971), p. 49ff.

15. Keith Melville, *Communes in the Counterculture* (New York: William Morrow, 1972), p. 170.

16. cf. Ron Roberts, *The New Communes* (Englewood Cliffs: Prentice-Hall, 1971).

17. cf. Katherine Kinkade, *Twin Oaks* (New York: William Morrow, 1972).

18. An interesting piece of recent research has shown that in comparison with other communes, utopian societies with religious foundations have survived much longer on the average. cf. Karen and Edward Stephan, "Religion and the Survival of Utopian Communities," *Journal for the Scientific Study of Religion* (March 1973), pp. 89-100.

19. James V. Cunningham, *The Resurgent Neighborhood* (Norte Dame: Fides Publications, 1965), p. 41.

20. cf. Donald and Rachelle Warren, "Six Kinds of Neighborhoods: Parochial, Diffuse, or Stepping-Stone?" *Psychology Today* (June 1975), pp. 74-81.

21. cf. Peter Berger's chapter on secularization in *The Sacred Canopy* (Garden City: Doubleday & Co., 1969). A similar but more satirical discussion of this phenomenon is offered by Edward Fiske, "The Selling of the Deity," *Saturday Review of Education* (Jan. 1973), pp. 17-19.

22. cf. Leonard Schapiro, *Totalitarianism* (New York: Praeger, 1972), p. 36f.

23. Robert Nisbet, *Tradition and Revolt* (New York: Random House, 1968), p. 136.

24. cf. Dean Kelly, *Why Conservative Churches are Growing* (New York: Harper & Row, 1972).

CHAPTER 5

The Family of God

> "Choosing a family used to be uninteresting. It is, today, an act of intelligence and courage."
> —Michael Novak

The recovery of tradition in the post-affluent era will not ensue, however, with the rehabilitation of humanity's most ancient, venerable, and elemental institution -- the family. This prognosis may seem either quaint or hackneyed nowadays when sociological folklore assumes the steady and irreversible disappearance of family life in the Western world. Not only does the demise of the family merit scarcely a shrug in light of the latest statistics on divorce rates, child abandonment, single parenting and so forth, but many of the more vocal critics of contemporary society at large, especially feminists, shed few tears for its passing. They heap it among the charnel of such noxious historical institutions and practices as slavery and child labor. Novelists, playwrights, and film-makers over the last several decades have belabored the themes of family-breakup, of protracted guerilla warfare between mates, of sibling enmity. One can think of such burlesques of domesticity as Albee's *Who's Afraid of Virginia Wolff?*, Pinter's *The Homecoming*, or Bergman's *Portrait of a Marriage*. Radical feminists such as Germain Greer, Ti-Grace Atkinson, or Caroline Bird have flayed the "patriarchal" heritage of Western family relations and called for the abolition of the conjugal norm as a necessary first step in emancipating the second sex. They, as well as other social revolutionaries, have reiterated the view of Marx and Engels that the family in capitalist society is little more than a product of class domination -- a convenient means for protecting property and for exploiting women and children in amassing profit. Thus justice demands the liquidation of the family along with large banks and corporations. Radical psychologists such as R. D. Laing and David Cooper have intimated that the family is primarily a political institution which, like the military and the schools, brutalizes human beings, makes them subject to interpersonal and social conflicts they cannot handle, and ultimately drives them to madness.[1] Sociologists continue publishing empirical studies of the disintegration of the family, thus giving weight to the not uncommon feeling that what has generally been the case up to now probably will be the case in the future.

In all fairness to those who malign the family's prospects it must be pointed out that many of the flaws which they perceive in the family nowadays are genuine. The erosion of family solidarity, especially since the Second World War, has not been due to the stridency of the institutions' detractors alone. Nor has the women's liberation movement been as guilty of undermining the family structure as conservatives from William Buckley to Marabel Morgan have contended. The family fell into disarray well before certain disgruntled professional women and choleric academics decided to debunk it. By and large the target of the critics has been that unstable, yet persistent arrangement known as the "nuclear family," consisting of husband, wife, and children minus grandparents or other relatives.

Unfortunately, the rhetoric against the nuclear family has frequently tended to damn unduly its contemporary variation and to romanticize earlier kinds of interpersonal relationships.[2] Disillusionment with the insular American middle-class family has swollen into a broadside against the family as a human institution *per se*. It is a sad fact that so many prophets of the family's doom betray an unconscionable ignorance of historical and anthropological research into the evolution of family life through time.

On the other hand, many of the popular arguments in the family's defense suffer the same myopia. The "family" frequently championed by moralists, journalists, and politicians amounts to little more than that of the husband as an absentee breadwinner, the wife as a compliant bed-partner and housekeeper, and the children as scrubbed little middle-class minions of the Dick and Jane variety. Such mythology, recited in comic strips and television comedies, has been the magnet of the women's movements' wrath and public sentimentality. The nuclear, middle-class family has been given more credit than is due, and we may at least commend the radicals for having tried to keep the debate as honest as possible. But if the radicals have shown us that the "Father Knows Best" and "Leave it to Beaver" idylls were mostly fluff, they have not yet convinced us that the counter image of the obtuse and withdrawn husband with his "macho" complex to preserve, along with the long-suffering, frustrated and unfulfilled wife, accurately depicts the typical family in contemporary culture. The problem of the family today is much more searching and complex than the rhetoric suggests.

The Affluent Family

The "sickness" of the family in recent times can be understood less as some mysterious, moral pathology than as the adaptation of the institution itself to industrial society and to the growth of affluence. Historically, the question of the viability of the institution seems to have arisen in the nineteenth and twentieth centuries when the family gradually lost much of its social utility and could no longer be taken for granted. As modern historians of the family are painfully aware, early written documents took little notice of changes and nuances in domestic relationships, simply because they were not considered important. On the other hand, the latter day critique of family customs and values has unleashed immense study and scholarship on them. We take the history and sociology of the family so seriously because the family is no longer presumed natural and inevitable.[3]

In past centuries the family played a more indispensible biological, economic, or cultural role than it does now. It furnished the context in which the young of the species, whose long maturation period required a stable environment for nurture and physical security, could be reared. It allowed for financial co-operation and mutual work arrangements not only between spouses and children, but also between small groups related by blood. For instance, the pre-industrial farm family was something of a miniature society in its own right. Because of the need of the family to be self-sufficient in the production of the goods of life and because of the lack of a cash economy, several generations often dwelt together on the land and labored cooperatively. (The impact of a cash economy and opportunities for employment off the land undermined this arrangement and weakened family ties.)[4] Moreover, the family offered socially legitimate channels for the transmission of property and wealth, in so far as one's inherited holdings were an important gauge of class and status as well as the basis of a livelihood. This was as true in ancient Rome as in colonial America. Finally, the family served as the fulcrum of traditional life. It was the chief source of education and the main agent of socializing children before the arrival of public institutions for accomplishing the same purpose. Romantic attachments between mates, as well as the emphasis on affection between children and parents, were either

inconsequential or subordinate to the practical value of
the family as an organ of social solidarity. In most
archaic cultures the "family" is principally a web of
kinship bonds embracing both the dead and the unborn,
and one's identity as a person is defined by these bonds.
Domestic hearths with "eternal flames," as well as rituals
for worshipping the spirits of ancestors, are tokens of
the family as an intimate universe in which the person's
life, now and in the hereafter, is circumscribed. Even
in the industrial Japan of the twentieth century, family
members participate in a network of duties and responsibilities encompassing loyalty to community, employer, emperor,
and nation.

While generalizations pitting the "modern" family
against its "ancient" or pre-industrial counterparts are
always risky, it is fair to say that the notion of family
as something which binds and constitutes an individual
through kinship or community involvements has elapsed.
The contemporary ideal of the family focuses first on the
needs of the husband and wife, then on those of the children,
and only tangentially on those of relatives and society,
if at all. The contemporary family is more a *convenient
alliance* for companionship and respectability and though
to a diminishing degree, for sex and the security of children. The marriage partnership thus has come to be
validated almost exclusively with regard to the compati-
bility of the couple. It rests on the romantic notion
of two separate persons united by similar intersts and
emotions. If individual needs, however, are not satisfied
in the marriage, the union is thought to be a failure,
and divorce may ensue. The reigning social values behind
contemporary motives for marriage, therefore, are the
standard middle-class concerns with self-actualization
and personal development, as a famous study by Weinstein

and Platt showed a number of years back.[5] Marriage is that sanctuary for personal needs, supposedly immune from social pressures and especially the promptings of parents. The "happiness" of the individual is its sole *raison d'être*. This requirement, of course, frees the individual from threats to his own autonomy and leaves the marriage as a refuge from the importunity of society. On the other hand, it makes the criteria of a successful marriage more difficult to meet and the friction from an awkward match intolerable. As Margaret Mead has observed wryly, "To all the other exorbitant requirements for a perfect mate must be added 'capacity to grow.'"[6]

The crisis of the family, therefore, has immediately to do with current attitudes toward family and society itself. The issue of the "nuclear family" as such is something of a red herring, since the character of the nuclear family nowadays manifests itself more in the way people feel about living with each other than in the physical composition of individuals under the same roof. As Phillipe Ariés, the eminent French historian of the family has surmised, the current nostalgia for the "extended" family as of a number of parents and grandparents occupying a single residence is more fancy than fact.[7] The nuclear module of husband, wife, and children persisted even in those societies which saw the family as embracing distant blood relations in a sharing of mutual economic tasks and a common story. The difference between the families of today and yesterday is as much a matter of psychology as of living space. A rural American family in the nineteenth century identified itself not so much by geographical nearness (the westward migrations often caused a greater physical separation of generations than is the case even presently) as by the sentiment "looking out for one's own." Aunt Sally in

far away Ohio could expect help from her kin in Kansas if
trouble arose. Even as late as 1959, one important sociological study revealed that the "sense" of an extended
family survived in large measure among the lower and middle
classes in America.[8] Better transportation and communication enabled relatives to spread out geographically while
remaining in close and regular contact with each other. The
AT&T advertisements about loved ones being "as near as the
telephone" suggest how family connections need not depend
on the having of homes in the same town.

Yet there has been a conspicuous trend away from the
psychological associations of an extended family, despite
vestigial signs to the contrary. One sign is the growing
tendency to count within the family only those relatives
of direct lineage -- parents and grandparents and perhaps
a few aunts or uncles, with first and second cousins and
even in-laws omitted. The proliferation of divorces and re-
marriages has further confused the profile of the family,
while bringing into relief the shrinking number of individuals
who participate during their lifetime in a truly nurturing
group of intimates.

The nuclear family, for its part, no longer concerns
two who sleep together but two who genuinely know or care
to know one another. The interface between nuclear family
and the surrounding support groups who comprise the community has shrunk considerably, thus reducing the range of
persons with whom one anticipates relationships in any
form. The nuclear family has really become an atomized
family -- existing within certain legal constraints but
with no real internal cement to hold it together or to
make it a vital, social element.

The nuclear family owes its evolution to the economic
conditions of affluence and the fragmenting of social

institutions which have taken place at the same time. As
we have seen, affluence itself has corroded the enduring
institutions of society, breaking up once solid commitments into marginal and temporary compacts. Thus it
comes as little surprise that marriage and the family
would suffer the same effects as other institutions.
When there remains little social or economic reason for
people to enroll their lives together, the only defense
of such bonding can be the free "choice" of the partners
or the desire for "self-enrichment," "companionship,"
or what have you. The present fashion among some young
couples of making marriage a legal contract whose conditions are set down according to the preferences of the
participants rather than in conformance with the stricter
demands of civil law, a contract which can be "nullified"
if the conditions are not met, reflects the tendency to
view matrimony as a dispensible and custom-made arrangement. If John balks at helping Mary with the housework,
or Mary turns out not to like backpacking after all, the
terms of the covenant can be voided. What to a tradition-
alist may seem unusual or even downright frivolous
requirements for making marriage tenable are taken with
utmost seriousness in the new spirit of contractual liberty.

A best-selling book by the O'Neills entitled *Open
Marriage* sets forth how a marriage tailored to individual
life goals and preferences of each partner can be made to
work effectively. Accoding to the O'Neills, "Open marriage
is not an abstract ideal" but "a suggestion for rewriting
your contract into a viable life style according to your
individual needs."[9] Nowhere in their brief about open
marriage is there any commendation of the old-fashioned
ideas of conjugal duty, or marriage as an institution
benefiting or actually affecting anybody but the man and
woman. Even the notion of "fidelity" drops its ethical

overtones and becomes merely the task of striving to be honest or "open" in negotiating what each individual wants to do with his or her time. Marriages today are frequently subject to negotiation, since the impersonal constraints on the family of yesteryear are no longer strong. Government welfare agencies that support women and dependent children, together with the increased earning potential of former wives, makes one-parent families a more feasible venture than before. Sentiments of loyalty and vocation in marriage have given way to the expectation of economic luxury, "satisfaction" in sexual dealings, and myriad psychic rewards. People look for more *performance* out of a relationship, an imperative implanted in everyone's consciousness through the numerous articles in women's magazines and paperbacks with such teasing captions as: "What does your marriage *really* have going for you?" or "Ten ways to make your marriage dynamic and exhilarating." The trouble is that "performance" becomes an excessive requirement: people set stiffer and stiffer personal demands for themselves until they can no longer countenance their own natural imperfections and dismiss marriage itself as hazardous to their mental health.

The less socially compelling marriage and the family become the more precarious and unstable appear the institutions themselves. However, the unsettled character of current family life and the personal tragedies which attend it spring from the deeper crisis of Western society which we have been describing. In this century the decline of the family has been postulated frequently as a key to the collapse of occidental civilization. Such was the view of Carle Zimmerman, who in his landmark book, *Family and Civilization*, portrayed the fragmented, "atomistic" family of the modern world as an augury of decadence.[10] The atomistic family, according to Zimmerman, is the mere ghost of its proud ancestry. The family has been devastated by an unchecked individualism, which has bred anarchy, crime, and nihilism as social

consequences. Society inevitably falls apart because its
sturdiest brace, the family, has given way. Zimmerman,
lamentably, in explaining the emergence of the atomistic
family echoes Oswald Spengler's rather simplistic and
fatalistic conception of human history, as running through
cycles of glory and decline; he has therefore been
assailed for using family history as camouflage for a
kind of moral theology. Even though, by Zimmerman's
account, the mechanisms for change in family structure
are unnecessarily vague, his citation of the data about
decline cannot be easily dismissed. He is perhaps more
discerning and appreciably less gratuitous than critics
like Edward Shorter, who in his *The Making of the Modern
Family* offers a glib tribute to the "freedom" and autonomy
which the implicit morality of the contemporary family
has enshrined.[11] For Shorter, modernization, mobility,
and intransience are just simple historical wave movements
to which domesticity will naturally "adapt." As John
Crosby writes:

> The family is in a state of breakdown and
> decay. False. Which family? Whose family?
> Moralists and politicians seem to relish this
> theme... In recent years the family has under-
> gone changes in life style, leisure-time pursuits,
> mobility, method of communication, and intergener-
> ational relationships... Is this to be defined
> as breakdown? Divorce rates are higher than
> in previous decades. Does this mean that more
> marriages are failing or that more failing
> marriages are admitting the failure and doing
> away with the pretense? The family, in one
> variation or another, has survived for several
> thousand years. There is little question that
> it will continue to survive, perhaps evolving
> and changing, with variations in function and
> structure.[12]

In other words, there is no such thing as social disintegration, only social change. Change cannot be assigned

a negative value, for change is unequivocally good. Rome did not fall; it only underwent an extreme modification.

Social scientists, with their allergy for appraisal, rarely admit basic causes for change, and are even less willing to make a value judgment about them. But the relationship between the much discussed "changes" in the family and the compulsions of affluence can hardly be overlooked in any analysis of why such a time-honored social institution has buckled under stress. The issue is exactly how everyday human contacts, affinities, and allegiances are distorted for the sake of sustaining a high standard of living. We are all too familiar with the portrait of the corporate executive who trades nearly all of his family time for success on the job, while the stay-at-home wife languishes in their suburban brick box in Outer Oneonta. Bored, forlorn, stuck with the kids most of the day, and cut off from meaningful communication with her husband, she invests all her sense of identity in her role as homemaker, though with suppressed anger.[13] Often both husband and wife rationalize their sorry plight by telling themselves that such a style of living pays out in the end with the pleasures of the "good life." Clergy and psychiatrists encourage distraught women under these circumstances to be "grateful" to their men for making such "sacrifices" for them and the children. The age-old idea of familial duty, therefore, no longer serves to enforce monogamy, but gets twisted to sanction the acute specialization of sex roles necessary for both a high income and the upkeep of the home. The woman is expected to do the cleaning, shuttle the children from school to Cub Scouts, tend to the social calendar, so that the man can be free to pursue professional objectives. John Kenneth Galbraith has contended that the job of housewifery is the keel of our mass consumer culture.

Since men are so busily engaged in making money and producing goods, there must be a cadre of buying "experts" -- i.e., women -- whose regular occupation is to "administer" consumption. The morality of the affluent society, according to Galbraith, fosters the myth of the pampered and complacent housewife, insofar as it "ascribes virtue to what is really the convenience of the producers of goods."[14]

Prone to hyperbole, Galbraith's assessment nonetheless has a piercing edge to it. In the affluent society the supervision of the household has lost much of its direct social and economic importance, especially since the advent of small families, labor-saving conveniences, and the availability of outside services. Many chores and acitivities filling the hours of affluent wives are not done out of necessity but to give content to their lives or to improve on already redundant comforts. The Madison Avenue icon of the conscientious woman zealously waxing her floor to shimmering perfection, or yearning for her laundry to come out "whiter than white," or brewing impeccable coffee, cynically reflects the sly effort of media moguls to celebrate the banality of the housewife's routines. With lessening of the overall labor time for running the home, and with loss of its economic importance, have come a dearth in the status attached to domestic vocations. The overblown cult of domestic bliss, which peaked in the 1950's, may have been nothing more than a balm for those tied to an occupation already deprived of prestige. The emptiness of the housewife role has recently been proclaimed in the vehement diatribes of the women's liberation movements, and in their wake has come a drive for equality in the social functions of the sexes.

Some traditionalists have considered the equalization of sex roles a major threat to the fabric of the family. Though equalization has emerged as a response to the loss of genuine economic contributions by women, the breakdown of the family began in an earlier stage of modern social evolution through the isolation of individuals from kin and community, and the forfeiture of enduring family relationships in pursuit of power, prestige, mobility, and money. The affleunt family may very well be the source of the family's woes; and the decline of the family will only be halted when the worst features of affluence are removed. Unhappily, the assault on the nuclear family and the customary definitions of "women's place" by the new feminist movement has not really succeeded in probing to the heart of the matter, the underlying corruption of *all* human relations. In this respect the twilight of affluence may invite a thorough reconsideration of what men and women together, rather than women alone, *can* do instead of what they would *like* to do with their lives.

Affluence and the Ethos of Autonomy

It seems more and more that people would like to swear by the credo of the "new" autonomous person -- self-discovery, heightening of experience, success in an occupation, and independence from "entagling" interpersonal commitments. Or at least that is what many popular observers of the cultural scene would have us believe. The maxims of privatism and the nurture of individual potential have already been discussed in relation to the ideology of affluence, and it comes as no surprise that such values have come to shape attitudes toward the family as well. The doctrine of autonomy, versus a true recognition of interdependence and social involvement, has become the all-too-handy answer to the steady dissolution of natural links among persons and institutions. The difficulty is that such a doctrine has been patented as an irresistible mandate of contemporary civilization without recognition of its status as a sedative for the conscience of affluent, upper middle-class America. According to the doctrine, for example, people are no longer morally obliged to safeguard certain types of relationships with others or to express themselves sexually in a socially acceptable manner. People "prefer" to live either singly or connubially, to care for their children or entrust them to baby-sitters, to have intimacies with the same or opposite sex. (It is not polite to brand people as either "homosexual" or "heterosexual" any more. We speak only of sexual "preference.") Pure preferentiality, however, is the other side of privilege. Only those who have the economic means to behave or express themselves exactly as they want can deny obligation as a significant moral category and choose at will from a smorgasbord of values.

The ideology of the affluent, upper middle-class as it pertains to the family has been well documented by sociologists. We have already spoken of the value of pure preferentiality. A second is a kind of automatic commitment to change, including social change, which somehow must be always "for the good."[15] A third is a rejection of previous religious ideas of marriage as a sacred trust and a growing conviction that the merits of matrimony depend on every person's own special propensities.[16] A fourth is the subordination of marriage itself to career interest, coupled with the association of happiness with job position and success. A fifth is the premium placed on not getting tied down to one place, or by extension, to one person. Robert Coles has described it vividly: "The uprootedness of the upper middle-class...almost parallels the uprootedness of migrant farm workers. In both cases, families feel that they can't get too close to anything because they may be transferred -- told to move on."[17] Finally, the preoccupation with being mobile and fancy-free engenders preference for the fleeting and temporary and prompts the use of marriage as an expedient for having plenty of "experiences," including dinners in charming little restaurants, or companionship while on tour in South America.

The commendation of marriage as a spur to hedonistic and self-satisfying life-styles, together with the denigration of child-rearing, comes across quite strikingly in a book by Ellen Peck, *The Baby Trap*. In Peck's words, "Marriage should not signal a 'settling down,' but a waking up. Marriage is rather like a growing plant that should be enriched, fed with stimulating experiences from outside sources; if it is not, it will shrivel into boredom and routine."[18] Again the message is the *bon ton* of affluent elitism: the false dichotomy between the high life and dullness, between sensation and ennui. The difference between the ruling class mentality of America today and that of our grandparents is that the latter made a fetish of wealth and respectability. Today's ruling class rejects wealth, which it already has, for *la vie passionnante*. "We prefer," Peck says, "not to spend money on possessions and status gadgetry, but rather on experience and sensation." She adds: "And we do not have children. We do not want children."[19] One cannot live "deeply" and raise a family at the same time. Peck does not want to "learn about creative playthings, toilet training, and playground etiquette." She proclaims, unabashed: "I want the Riviera in January."[20]

Marriage is not only a convenience; it is a shopping cart in the supermarket of thrills and highs. The fact that Peck takes the high-bred verve of the jet set as somehow a model not only for marriage, but for the right style of living itself, is instructive of the values of the audience she writes for. We find the same implicit social assumptions in much popular psychology. For instance, Herbert Otto sees "the new marriage" as bringing "an emphasis on the cultivation of ecstasy and on the joyous celebration of life."[21] Otto contrasts the style of ecstasy with a couple's proneness to "boredom and satiation with each other" which "is made tolerable largely by the devotion and responsibility attendant to the upbringing of the children."[22] In the same volume as Otto's essay, Sidney M. Jourard notes the dependence of the "new marriage" on affluence. He writes that

> ...in America, the most affluent nation that ever existed, objective reasons for enforcing conformity are diminishing. At last, we have the power and the wealth (despite proteststions from conservative alarmist to the contrary) to ground *a fantastically pluralistic society*. Indeed, *not* to capitalize on our increased release from economic necessity, *not* to "play" creatively with such existential forms as marriage, family life, schooling, leisure pursuits, etc. is a kind of madness.[23]

Furthermore, "the family structure for the emerging age of affluence and leisure cannot be prescribed or described in advance -- only invented."[24] One wonders, however, about and what implications the present reversal in economic fortunes has for such a forecast. Perhaps one cannot talk so nonchalantly any more about toying with or inventing institutions when the economic basis of moral and social liberty is lacking.

Throughout all such rhetoric runs the presupposition that marriage is really nothing more than amusement for the well-off -- for those who can afford to be blasé and ceaselessly experimental. Not surprisingly, the working classes have never envisaged their options for marriage in such a way; and in most traditional societies where institutions serve to provide stability in work arrangements and in the family compact for the sake of economic security, the thesis that two people can have the prerogative of contriving a relationship and taking it apart at will would seem incomprehensible, if not outlandish. The new sensibility concerning the artificial character of male and female bonding makes marriage into a cheap commodity, and thereby dehumanizes those who in their hearts can probably not deny the emotional and physical interdependence of the sexes. The rallying cry for the so-called "liberated" couple is that marriage exploits individuals, especially women, in the service of the "system." Those who cling to the sentiment of "to death do us part" have really been "brainwashed" into accepting some form of unholy alliance which benefits selfish males, corporations, the power structure, or any other familiar spirit in the new popular, leftwing demonology. In response it certainly cannot be gainsaid that many affluent, upper middle-class marriages owe their very purpose to the adoration of the god Mammon. The trouble comes when those who realize that they have been participating in an unholy alliance, which damages women and children primarily, seek to absolve themselves of their class privileges and prejudices and decree marriage to be unhealthy for all. They offer us, furthermore, the "universal" alternative: a world where everybody can be independent, well-situated, and free to attain private gratifications.

It may be hard for one who has recoiled from boredom in an affluent marriage to realize that many couples of lesser means might envy the opportunity to be "bored." Many lower-class marriages hang together because the man and woman share daily the same burden of deprivation and the struggle to cope. Though historically there have been more divorces and family abandonments among the lower-class than within the upper strata of society, the reason has little to do with the "boredom" and routine of marriage. Rather, lower-class unions come apart because chronic unemployment and poverty cause unbearable strains on both sides. The well-known absence of the father in welfare families is a case in point. Frequently the father "has" to leave because he cannot earn enough to support the children, and the wife can do better on welfare.

With respect to middle class marriages there is some evidence that hard times, while putting stress on family relations initially, tends to strengthen commitments over time. Thus the rate of marital breakups sank dramatically during the Great Depression. As Stouffer and Lazarsfeld have surmised: "It might be possible to cite numerous examples, from case histories, of couples (in the Depression) whose conflicts normally would have ended in divorce, yet whose inability to pay for divorce forced them to weather the crisis and whose experience led to mutual understanding and harmony."[25] The loss of an economic surplus in family budgets, for example, probably induced husbands and wives to do more things together, rather than separately, thus promoting solidarity.[26] In fine, affluence conditions people to look at marriage in terms of its margin-utility and hence its *disposibility;* the waning of affluence moves them to the necessity of marriage for the protection of its members and thus a possible stimulus to feelings of shared responsibility that may deepen into love. The need for commitment ensures recognition of the *reality* and value of such a commitment.

Jessie Bernard has remarked that in connection with divorce "the trend nowadays is no longer to think in terms of violation of a commitment but in terms of incompatibility, a state of affairs rather than a violation of a promise."[27] Incompatibility becomes a congenital ailment in a culture where abundance and competing options for living raise people's expectations for themselves so far that it turns out to be exceedingly difficult to reconcile personal differences. The limiting of options, while regrettable from the standpoint of those who prize individual potential and autonomy over all other values, can actually rebound to the benefit of fundamental social commitments, and make the sanctity of covenants or promises appear not so easily negotiable. If the covenant is broken, the consequences cannot be so lightly dismissed. The sanctity of covenants rests on the more basic commitment of both parties to guarantee "justice" in the relationship. On the other hand, the lack of justice in the contemporary marriage contract has eroded confidence in the institution itself, and helping to set off the contemporary women's rebellion.

Women's Liberation and the Family

Exactly what this default on justice is has been disputed even by that checkered group who are modern marriage's foremost critics -- the new feminists. Their more extreme and vitriolic representatives are similar to similar to Ruth Dickinson, who calles herself a "misogamist" and a "feminist" for whom marriage is "the most damaging force our species has ever invented."[28] Out of this cast of mind has arisen the mythology of many radical women which brands matrimony as a universal form of slavery in which the female becomes the male's chattel. Susan Brownmiller in her book on rape has adopted something of this line, and it has been echoed in other widely read feminist diatribes, particularly the writings of Kate Millett and Germaine Greer.[29] Those who resort to such a mode of argument delight in taking examples from patriarchal cultures where brides could be bought and sold, and rape was a kind of "theft."

The less polemical elements in the women's liberation movements do not bank on weak historical analogies or indictments of global male conspiracies; nor do they condemn marriage outright. They focus on the manner in which women today suffer real hardship and psychological pains because of the circumstances of many marriages. Writers such as Elizabeth Janeway point a crucial finger at the isolation of women in middle-class homes, and the denial to children of "a variety of adult role models," a denial springing from the persistence of the absent career father and the lonely vigil of the suburban housewife.[30] Janeway focuses on the truncation of family and social relations under conditions of affluence. The challenge of the women's movement, in this context, is that of reconfirming the lost family partnership between males and females in child-rearing and in work. The injustices to women today are not taken as some sinister manifestation of perennial male oppression, but as an outgrowth of the existing social and economic structure. Not only must there be an end to the isolation of the woman in the home from kin and community as well as husband; also overt discrimination against the female sex in job hiring and salary policies must cease -- in other words, there must be equal opportunity in employment and equal pay for equal work. In addition, the work system must be redesigned to permit a greater sharing of responsibilities in caring for children as well as more flexible job schedules including maternity and paternity leaves, the availability of part-time work for both sexes, and day care facilities at places of employment. Altogether, most of these proposals constitute urgent and sensible ways of bringing the modern family back together, of integrating it once again with daily life in the community, and of ending the alienation of middle-class women which has not been appreciated enough by men for its dangerous, explosive potential.

On the other hand, the women's movement also runs the risk of legitimating, under the pretext of changing the lot of all women as a single class, the values and distinctive privileges of more affluent women. Leaders of the movement heatedly repudiate all charges of special interest, but sober inspection of the language of their manifestoes and demands prompts such conclusions. As with all bourgeois reform crusades, there is a tendency in the new feminist movement to fix on symbols of oppression which supposedly transcend economic factors and which excuse middle-class women from accountability for their own participation in the moral failures of our time. The mistreatment of one sex by the other under various guises does not leave *all* women *totally innocent victims* any more than it does men.

For instance, it is no mystery that the vanguard of the new feminism has been a growing legion of college-educated, career-oriented women. This fact in itself does not undercut the authentic aspirations of middle-class females, but it does suggest that the ultimate objectives of the movement have to be accepted for what they are. The demand that many women are making for an end to demeaning social stereotypes and sexual exploitation through media advertising, books, magazines, and folklore deserves most serious attention. That the ability to work at a meaningful and productive occupation is necessary to secure dignity and control one's own life has been seized upon by the feminist consciousness in assailing the traditional role of woman as man's unpaid servant. Yet careerism by itself has its own built-in pitfalls. To be sure, there are protestations that the women's movement is interested in raising the regard, and dealing with the problems, of females in even the lowest economic sectors of society. Yet the glamorous image of the successful professional, administrative, or executive person ranks first in the movement's repertoire of approved role models -- what we might call the "Brenda Starr syndrome." At the same time, the role of housewife, though given lip service as an "alternative" that some women freely and genuinely select, is subtly disparaged. The findings of sociologist Lotte Bailyn give force to the suspicion that the ideal of the "working woman" is related to education and professional training. Not only is "a woman's education...strongly related to the likelihood of her working," Bailyn discovered, but "the higher the professional qualifications of a woman, the more likely she is to be working."[31] If this were not the case, it must be asked, why would so many middle-class women be upset about wearing the badge of "housewife?" The emphasis on salaried careers in prestige posts contributes to the recurrent degrading of the less educated life and work style in our society, and stirs the seething pot of class tensions, a fact which many feminists would probably not like to admit. It is one thing for highly trained and skilled upper middle-class women to want equal access to the prerequisites of their social station; it is quite another to insist that the higher tokens of status be emulated by all women, thereby instilling feelings of inferiority among those whose circumstances do not allow the same sort of drive and achievement. The increasing resistance among some women to the Equal Rights Amendment and to the women's movement in general, while alarming because of its misplaced emotionalism, may in part be a response.

Caroline Bird, one of the "pioneers" in the latest surge of feminist advocacy, disclosed in an early book the class coloring of the women's movement, though without specific apology. Concerning the feminist goal of autonomy or "self-determination" for women, Bird avowed:

> The idea of self-determination is aristocratic. New Feminist women are so often frankly upper-class that they seem snobbish. Advertising, television, and popular magazines ignore them on the grounds that there aren't enough of them to matter. But if you want to know what's going to happen in the future, you must pay them very serious attention indeed. Their life style will become more common when more women are given a change to do what they want.[32]

Bird banked on the spread of affluence as a spur to take women out of the home, and offered the argument that economic growth

overall is somehow impeded by barring them from careers, as
implied in the subtitle of her book, "The High Cost of Keeping
Women Down." For Bird the solution to woman's underprivilege
is simply to give them the right to imitate their careerist
husbands. "All the measurable data -- vital statistics,
education, job patterns -- indicate that women will increasingly
find themselves living in ways that parallel rather than comment
the lives of their husbands."[33] Bird's analysis of the aspirations of women "in general," however, was based on interviews
with *Vassar graduates*, and she seemed to think that the careerist mentality evinced by such young women (a mentality which
excluded family) was somehow the key to generating a "revolutionary" strike force of an awakened femininity. In other
words, women should not be deprived of the opportunity to act
like power brokers and pace setters *a la* the while, upper
middle-class male. Bird declared categorically: "It is wrong
to deny individuals born female the right to inconvenience their
families to pursue art, science, power, prestige, money, or
even self-expression, in the way that men in pursuit of these
goals inconvenience their families as a matter of course."[34]
The intended criticism did not fall on men who "inconvenience"
their families, nor on the questionable value-scheme which does
not discriminate among the pursuit of "art" or "power" or
"money." Nor was there any suggestion that women seek, as a
bona fide revolutionary impulse, to remedy existing social
habits and priorities. So far as Bird was concerned, the issue
is the barring of women from a place in the careerist, male-
world of affluent living. It concerns not whether there should
be spoils; it concerns should have the right to roister with
them.

    Bird's appeal sounded a bit strident at times, but it
foreshadowed the larger principles and policy recommendations
of the magazine *MS.* and the National Organization of Women (NOW).

Both organs of opinion and action resemble each other inasmuch as they present the same profile of the "liberated woman." NOW has come to schism over the issue of implicit elitist biases. The debate has centered on whether NOW should push for the public recognition of lesbianism (an objective suiting the logic of "free sexual preference") and the upgrading of female employment, or pay more attention to the more conservative values and priorities of the less-educated and job-trained segment of the American female population. One faction has resisted the leadership of NOW and sought to bring the organization to work on behalf of less ideological matters and more toward resolution of "basic" legal or bread-and-butter issues, such as an end to overt discrimination in hiring, and equitable salaries for women who work.

Whether NOW truly represents the thinking of a genuine cross-section of American women, or whether it has an upper middle-class tinge, can be argued at some length. It can be claimed, however, that the problem of justice for women becomes detached in the rhetoric from other fundamental social and economic concerns. For example, NOW and much of the new feminist advocacy have supported the establishing of free day care for all children. The premises behind this political plank are several. They include the notions that (1) free child care would allow women who could otherwise not afford it to work; (2) it would alleviate the customary female burden of taking care of children; (3) it would guarantee women freedom from sole child nurturing roles as a right instead of as some dubious privilege. Outside of the expected right-wing recriminations there has been little opposition, in general, to the idea that free day care of their children should be provided for those working mothers who cannot pay for it themselves.

Whether it should be provided for all mothers has not been seriously addressed. Obviously, no day care can ever be "free." Day care would have to be paid for from public moneys or from tax revenue. In periods of economic scarcity, is it right, for affluent families to have the same social claim as lower income ones in the allocation of public moneys? Should there be an adjustment in the taxation of the wealthy to finance day care for the poor? Or should free day care be available only up to certain income levels? Many feminists would reply "no" to each question, since they perceive the primary issue to be the "rights of women," *not* the distribution of wealth in society or the prerogatives of certain classes versus others. Nevertheless, to grant free day care to all families regardless of income would boost the joint purchasing power of upper middle-class professional families even more by an equivalent to another notorious tax loopholes for the rich.

The creation of free day care open to all, furthermore, would not help to stem the ravages wrought on family living. The malaise affecting today's family has its source in a society which rates production and consumption over values, which sacrifices human relationships to the competitive itch for gain and status expressed in careerism. The abandonment of women by men who have succumbed to the Circean spell of careerism does not have to elicit imitation of their ways by women. To make it easier for women to embark on the same pursuits as men may be fair after the fashion of a devil's bargain. But the real imperative is to dismantle the economic and social structure which rewards careerist energies at the expense of family continuity. Many men, balking at the feminist programs, worry about the ruin of the family, when it is the very work commitments of the careerist male which has caused so great a ruin. The task of reform should proceed toward the reconstruction of the family, and that means more than awarding

women economic parity with men in the upper income bracket.
It means a rediscovery of the equality and mutual interdependence of the sexes in child nurturing, breadwinning, and in service to the community. It means turning our backs on the self-justifying individualist ideologies infecting both conservative and liberal commentaries on the family, and returning to a new respect for the family unit as not only the bond of social order, but the sphere in which the fulfillment of personal existence takes place.

The Family of God

To suggest that the family can have redemptive significance for both society and the individual is nothing world-rattling or novel. It is a commonplace that in one guise or another has informed the body of social beliefs in many cultures from age to age. Perhaps only in this century has such a commonplace drawn such widespread suspicion, even outside certain militant social philosophies like anarchism or Marxism. The modern origin of the radical's attack on the family has been the historical relationship between kinship and privilege, between blood loyalties and social oppression. Thus the socialists of the nineteenth century inveighed against the bourgeois family as a vehicle for monopolizing wealth and for controlling the means of production in industry. After 1949, the Maoists undertook to destroy the old, feudal, and patriarchal character of the Chinese family in order to eliminate the power of landlords and the fragmentation of political order which stood in the way of moving society toward the goals of the "revolutionary masses." The grinding poverty of the peasant classes, the Maoists saw, could never be eliminated unless the people's aspirations were deflected from selfish, small-group interests. The ancient, protective function of the family was abolished and replaced by the administrative reach of the state and the local commune.

On the other hand, in modern Western society the family has already relinquished most of its protective function, and the weakening of its influence and authority is an accomplished fact. But the breakdown of the modern Western family has not smoothed the way for either the reorganization of society or the genuine freedom of the person. It has left the lone individual prey to social competition and conflict, his own egotistical obsessions, and the instrusions of the corporate bureaucracy. Betty Yorburg has declared: "The family is the only area of life in industrial society that is not bureaucratized."[35] Yet the family has shrunk considerably in its importance as a center of meaning in people's lives, and the values of family life have steadily weakened before the wants or amibtions of individuals in the wider social arena. The family has been removed from participation in community activities; it has become idealized as a kind of oasis of equanimity amidst the "rat race," a retreat in which the harassed breadwinner can relax with pipe and slippers or "unwind" after a brutal workday.[36] Or the family has come to be perceived, especially by women, as a barrier to entrance into the mainstream of society which is "where the action is." To get rid of the family altogether, or to put its socializing and nurturing function into the hands of the state, as some feminists would prefer, would only complete the trend toward social fragmentation and the subjugation of the individual either to his own whims or the rule of the corporate bureaucracy.

Clearly, the restoration of the family as a sturdy ligature in a new society stitched together with shared

traditions and moral commitments would be a far more
revolutionary act than its abolition. Affluence has
damaged the family by inviting us to conceive the meaning of life in terms of abstract, individual ends such
as abundance, independence, or the "bitch goddess" success.
The business economist, James Kuhn, observes that modern
industrial society is "so concerned with production and
output that... (it can) evaluate changes in work activities or home life only as they may affect (a) limited
concept of production."[37] The end of affluence counsels
new thoughts, not only about the ultimate impracticability
of these ends, but also about our inability to rationalize
our infatuation with them, and about the possibility that
there are more gripping moral purposes to which we may
bind our maxims. Though the end of affluence spell the
loss of our power to acquire things, or to enjoy the
garnering of ever new sensations, it could bring back
to our attention the worth and fecundity of fundamental
human relationships. Also, should it make us realize
anew the reality of human interdependence, it could accent
the interdependence of the sexes and of the generations.

In the past the primacy of the family has been expressed
in the sacred aura with which societies have invested it.
It has been not just the biological necessity of the family,
but also its preserving of social cohesion and its fostering
of unique psychological satisfactions that have moved human
beings to cherish and revere it. The symbols of family union
have woven their way into the myths and metaphysics of the
world's religious legacies. They have been incorporated,
for example, into the Christian language of God as "father"
and the human race as his "children." In Jewish ritual,
according to Jacob Neusner, "The most intimate occasion
is the marriage ceremony."[38] The pairing of bride and
bridegroom constitute something of much greater consequence

than a practical social match. The vow of marriage suggests the eternal covenant between God and his people, indeed, a pact with the entire universe. In many archaic religions the *hieros gamos*, or "sacred marriage" between a god and goddess, represents the conjunction of opposites occuring with the creation of the cosmos. The family relationship, and in particular the marriage tie, therefore offers clues in the minds of many peoples of the past for the innermost significance of the human predicament. "What God has joined together, let no man put asunder" stands for something more than a casual social affiliation.

The loss of the sacred sense of marriage and the family is not irrecoverable in the same way as is the reverence for the old deities and myths that have dropped into the historical garbage bin. Specific religious or mythical notions of the family will certainly have to be abandoned, particularly those consigning women to vassal status, given the passing of pre-industrial society and its male-dominated hierarchy of power and morality. Yet the family itself will remain -- an intimate ensemble of primal and sensitive relationships between persons, a stage on which the perennial theatrics of love and hate, treachery and fidelity, are enacted and re-enacted. If Sigmund Freud was right -- not about his theories of sexual conflict and maturation, but about the importance of family experience for the molding of the human psyche -- then the future career of the family will continue to have definite effects on the self-understanding of every one of us. Moreover, in the womb of the family will grow new civilizations.

The new order that is dawning, as we have stressed, will *require* the institutionalizing of human interdependence. From finely knit seams and fibers of the family institution can extend threads that will mesh with the cords of social relationships -- laws, contracts, the rules of commerce, the canons of justice. An egalitarian society will be mirrored in a democratic family, and vice-versa. A culture with traditions will be contained and passed on through the family and community intercourse. More will be said about these prospects later.

The bane and delight of family living arise from our own expectations or definitions of what makes a whole human being, or what conduces to the spearing of that evasive trophy we call "happiness." It was Tolstoy who said that "all happy families resemble each other." The happy family with its whole personalities, therefore, becomes a reflection of the whole society. But for individuals to rediscover their own happiness in the family will require a different attitude toward the nature of happiness itself.

NOTES TO CHAPTER 5

1. R. D. Laing, *The Politics of the Family and Other Essays* (New York: Random House, 1972).

2. The notion of a primitive, matriarchal collective or communal fellowship known as the "extended family," is an example of such romanticizing.

3. For an excellent discussion of the problems of academic scholarship on the family, see Christopher Lasch, "The Family and History," *New York Review of Books* Nov. 13, 1975a), p. 33-38.

4. See Lucy Mair, *Marriage* (Balitmore: Penguin Books, 1971), p. 200.

5. See Fred Weinstein and Gerald Platt, *The Wish To Be Free* (Berkeley: University of California Press, 1961).

6. Margaret Mead, *Male and Female* (New York: William Morrow & Company, 1949), p. 361.

7. See Jacques Mousseau's interview with Phillipe Ariés, "The Family: Prison of Love," *Psychology Today* (August 1975), p. 75.

8. See M. B. Sussman, "Isolated Nuclear Family: Fact or Fiction?" *Social Problems* (Sprint 1959), p. 40.

9. Nena and George O'Neill, *Open Marriage* (New York: Harper & Row, 1947). p. 43.

10. See Carl Zimmerman, *Family and Civilization* (New York: Harper & Row, 1947).

11. Edward Shorter, *Making of the Modern Family* (New York: Basic Books, 1975).

12. John Crosby, *Illusion and Disillusion: The Self in Love and Marriage* (Belmont, Calif.: Wadsworth Publishing Co., 1973), p. 124-5.

13. This is a common scenario which is, however, refuted in a noted sociological study by H. C. Spectorsky, "The Exurbanites," in Bernard Rosenberg (ed.), *Analysis and Contemporary Society* (New York: Thomas Crowell, 1967).

14. John Kenneth Galbraith, *Economics and the Public Purpose* (New York: Houghton Mifflin, 1973), p. 227.

15. See David A. Schulz, *The Changing Family: Its Function and Future* (Englewood Cliffs, N.J.: Prentice-Hall, 1972), p. 158.

16. Schulz, p. 163.

17. Robert Coles, "The Cold, Tough World of the Affluent Family, *Psychology Today* (Nov. 1975), p. 70.

18. Ellen Peck, *The Baby Trap* (New York: Bernard Geis Associates, 1971), p. 7.

19. Peck, p. 8.

20. *ibid.*

21. Herbert A. Otto, "The New Marriage," in H. Otto (ed.), *The Family in Search of a Future* (New York: Appleton-Century-Crofts, 1970), p. 116.

22. Otto, p. 113.

23. Sidney M. Jourard, "Reinventing Marriage: The Perspective of a Psychologist," in *Otto,* op. cit., p. 46.

24. Jourard, p. 49.

25. Samuel A. Stouffer and Paul F. Lazarsfeld, *Research Memorandum on the Family in the Depression,* reprinted edition (New York: Arno Press, 1972), p. 72.

26. Stouffer, p. 922.

27. Jessie Bernard, *The Future of marriage* (New York: World Publishing Co., 1972), p. 93.

28. Ruth Dickenson, *Marriage as a Bad Habit* (Los Angeles: Sherborne Press, 1960), p. 17.

29. See Kate Millett, *Sexual Politics* (Garden City, NY: Doubleday & Co., 1970);
Germain Greer, *The Female Eunuch* (New York: McGraw Hill, 1971). The recent best-selling book by Susan Browmiller, *Against Our Will* (New York: Simon & Schuster, 1975) is of interest also in this connection.

30. See Elizabeth Janeway, *Between Myth and Morning* (New York: William Morrow, 1974).

31. Lotte Bailyn, "Family Constraints on Woman's Work," in Ruth Kundsin, *Women and Success* (New York: William Morrow, 1974), p. 95.

32. Carolyn Bird, *Born Female* (New York: David McKay, 1968), p. 147.

33. Bird, p. 148.

34. Bird, p. 200.

35. Betty Yorburg, *The Changing Family* (New York: Columbia University Press, 1973), p. 193.

36. See in this connection an interesting article by Kirk Jeffrey, "The Family as Utopian Retreat from the City: The Nineteenth Century Contribution," in Sallie TeSelle, *The Family, Communes, and Utopian Societies* (New York: Harper & Row, 1972).

37. Sydney Thomson Brown and James Kuhn, "Working Women and the Male Workday," *Christianity & Crisis* (Feb. 21, 1977), p. 30.

38. Jacob Neusner, *The Way of Torah* (Belmont, California: Dickenson Publishers, 1970), p. 13.

CHAPTER 6

The Pursuit of Happiness

"In this democracy it has become a public
duty to be as happy as one can be."

--Dorothy Thompson

Any reappraisal of the future of American society nowadays inevitably touches on the themes struck by our nation's celebration of its 200th birthday. The question arises as to the relationship between the altered conditions of life in the twilight of affluence -- the historical ideals of the Republic, and the popular aspirations of the American people. As we have already stressed, the new era will call forth an extensive examination of many treasured assumptions, particularly the notion of a lasting, boundless prosperity for all. Material boon for the masses of our citizens, even if not guaranteed explicitly in the Constitution, constitutes an unwritten promise of our heritage. The opportunity for constant improvement in one's circumstances is intimated in the opening lines of the Declaration of Independence, which calls for "life, liberty, and the pursuit of happiness." Throughout the generations the phrase "pursuit of happiness," however murky in its original philosophical import, has been construed by many as a charter for all to partake without restriction in the good life. Thomas Jefferson amended the initial wording of the Declaration, which employed John Locke's language of "life, liberty, and property," with the

expression "pursuit of happiness" in order to bestir
the revolutionary ardor of the common people. Jefferson
himself reflected many years thereafter that such wording
as contained in the Declaration "was intended to be an
expression of the American mind."[1] The ethic of the
pursuit of happiness, therefore, was established at the
outset as the casting weight of American democracy.

Regardless of what Jefferson himself intended by the
concept, the pursuit of happiness has been invoked repeatedly to justify the American desire for personal well-being.
Advocates of free enterprise have used it as a safeguard
against government interference in their quest for profit.
Leaders of the "People's Park" protest in Berkeley in 1969
recited those same words as a proof text for their claim
to grass-roots control over local facilities. Yet in the
main the pursuit of happiness has always been associated
in some general way with the endeavor to overcome economic
scarcity and raise every man's standard of living. David
Potter, in his book *People of Plenty*, has argued that
preoccupation with material abundance as the end of life
is profoundly embedded in the American character.[2] The
pursuit of happiness, in the sense of a never-ending
search for earthly riches and success, first manifested
itself, according to Potter, in the conquest of the
frontier -- in the myth of the bountiful wilderness to
be won and enjoyed. With the closing of the frontier
the myth was transmuted into confidence in a technological
cornucopia into faith in this country's scientific capacity
to ensure an ever-increasing life of ease and comfort.

Always happiness has been viewed not as a fixed quantity
but as a reserve of capital that could be enlarged indefinitely. In economic theory, such an attitude passed into
the neoclassical idea of the human being as a creature
with insatiable wants to be met as far as possible by

the productive capacity of industry. At the level of popular piety and morality, emphasis on the pursuit of happiness gave rise to a bewildering array of rationales for the enrichment of the individual. The prevalent ideal of personal self-fulfillment as the *summum bonum* of life, as well as the growing cult in religion and psychology of cultivating the "human potential," are only the most recent variations on this long-standing motif. In short, different versions of the "eudaimonistic" theory of value -- Aristotle's doctrine that every individual should strive to maximize his own happiness -- have flourished in a climate of optimism about the psychic and material rewards people deserve and what they can hope to attain.

Needless to say, the shrinking of affluence will force a general reappraisal of these goals of human existence. Individualism, eudaimonism, and even old-fashioned hedonism will have to be surveyed closely as to whether they are realistic moral strategies in an age demanding co-operation and resourcefulness for survival. It is a general lesson of history that the easier everyday living becomes, the more people take for granted the routines of simple getting and spending. By the same token, the more intense the search for new, exotic, and heightened experiences becomes. Heretofore, emancipation of the human race from the "curse of necessity," which has made possible the opening of the personality to the depths and treasures of self-awareness, has been considered an unquestioned good. The "challenge of leisure" has been touted by sociologists in the mid-twentieth century as the premier dilemma for the children of affluence. How to train the intellect and emotions to respond to an environment in which the biological and social agendas of work, raising a family, providing for others, are no longer written according to the same script for everybody, has been seen as the foremost task of the new age of economic freedom and security. What John Stuart Mill termed the "higher pleasures," possible only after basic needs are satisfied now become available to the butcher, the baker, and the candlestick maker. Yet all that may well demand revision if the job of meeting basic needs becomes a problem for society again. The tendency to take for granted the ordinary requirements of living may not be as morally or spiritually commendable as the siren song of affluence has bewitched us into believing. The pursuit of happiness may turn out to be less of a popular mandate and more of an outworn credo which, if perpetuated, will threaten the social order of the future.

Turning Down the Ecstatic

The pursuit of happiness in the 1960's and early 1970's evolved into a general obsession with the ecstatic -- and not just among the young. The point of life, many assumed, was to find the best ways of "getting high." To alter consciousness, or "tuning in to the good vibrations," was envisioned as the consummate aspiration of the new "revolutionary" spirit. The drug culture gave way to a new religiosity centering around meditation and mind-exploration techniques. The hawkers of this new sensibility reminded us that our "normal" perspective on the world was too prosaic, that we were too easily disposed to be unfeeling, dull-witted, conformist clods who rarely experience anything beyond our petty anxieties and trivial concerns. We were exhorted to snap out of our torpor, to get "outside" ourselves and encounter the "other" dimension of reality. Theodore Roszak in his book, *Where the Wasteland Ends*, following the Romantic visionaries of the nineteenth century, speaks of the need for a "rhapsodic intellect," whereby the "Reality Principle of the modern world" is "transformed" by reverie and the unconscious delights of dream-making.[3]

Similarly, Harvey Seifert, a theologian, has criticized those traditional religious doctrines and cultural mind sets which constrict human consciousness and deny people "a dependable gift of grace liberating them from the tyranny of convention and of material things."[4] Life, according to Seifert, must be "seen as an arena for enjoyment."[5] Such an enjoyment is decidedly transcendental, as Alan Watts proclaimed for years. The *via contemplativa* (the "contemplative way") becomes a magnificent opening to all the sensations of a universe that cannot be experienced by the average drone and drudge. The *via activa* (the way of active engagement with our physical surroundings and of problem-solving) which has dominated our modern technocratic life-styles no longer has much worth. "Reality," wrote Watts, "is what exists without effort."[6] The assumption is that authentic experience stems from the blessings of leisure. The "new" person of the future will divest himself of all survival mechanisms and social controls on both thought and action in order to revel in the miraculous moment.

By and large the new evangel of ecstasy has been promoted as an alternative to the pursuit of happiness regarded as a struggle to amass personal property and possessions. The style of conduct which the new evangel implies is nonacquisitive; it urges us to scout for happiness in our inner spirit alone. Difficulty, however, lies with the implicit consequences of such a style. As we saw earlier, any theology of the free-spirit, like the theology of play or a theology of ecstasy, has affluence as a prerequisite along with its ethic of uninhibited individualism, so that the drama of daily coping does not rally much attention. In order to perceive the more subtle music of the cosmos, we must be spared our daily nuisances and petty worries, primarily by having somebody else relieve us of them. To put the matter somewhat uncharitably, every guru must have a charwoman to wash his socks in the evening; every full-time devotee of the inner radiance must have a valet to put his supper on the table. That is why old, sprawling estates with musty stables and wooded grounds are common locales for various ventures in consciousness expansion. Though not making material sufficiency an end, the pursuit of ecstasy presupposes it as a vital means to an end.

Bertrand Russell once observed that the more munificent a person's manner of living, the more he requires unique forms of excitement to remain content. When the business of merely "getting by" is rendered superfluous because of heightened material well-being, a person's energies are directed toward more refined interests. Similarly, ease of satisfying minimal needs weakens familial and communal bonds which historically have served as guarantees that sparse rewards will be distributed equitably, that hardship will be shared to some extent. The psychic individualism of those immersed in the pursuit of ecstasy can be a live option only when other social claims are not made upon them -- when there is nothing to distract from the unfettered fondling of the frontal lobes. Repudiation of overt pleasure-seeking by proponents of the new spirituality is compromised by their dependence on extraneous wealth which frees them from materialistic entanglements. If, as Philip Slater suggests, "the new culture is founded on a rejection of scarcity assumptions," [7] then the reappearance of scarcity must undermine the prospects for happiness in such a culture. An enforced cutback of life's conveniences coming with hard times, rather than the supposedly "voluntary" renunciation of the goods of this world by those jaded with them, will involve styles of experiencing that can hardly be imagined by those now bent on personal rapture and the civilization of immediate feelings.

The problem will all recipes for mass ecstasy, though, is that they do not really solve the problem of happiness. The genuinely ecstatic occurs only in a rare moment of illumination, is unbidden, and cannot be domesticated as an everyday mode of experience. The great religious breakthroughs of history, the revelations or enlightenments precipitating new teachings and living traditions, on the main were sudden and incomparable events in which the meaning of human existence was clarified in dramatic fashion. The same can be said for many of the experiences of the classical mystics: rather than simply consisting in blissful rapture, such experiences brought with them a complete revaluation of the aspirant's former habits and perspectives. Luther started a Reformation; Saint Francis gave up his worldly patrimony. In such instances it was not a matter of discovering new routes of "enjoyment." Faith and wisdom are more important qualities of genuine ecstasy than happiness.

We may contrast the world-transfiguring character of genuine ecstasy with the cheapening of the ecstatic in contemporary culture. At bottom the cult of ecstasy today merely follows the quest for constant gratification which ties in with the narcissism of the affluent. The sensuality, for example, of contemporary youth is readily translated into the artistry of "mind-blowing" outlined by transpersonal psychologists and popular mystics as glibly and mechanically as the gambits of lovemaking in a sex manual. Whereas authentic ecstasy comes from humility, cheap ecstasy is engineered by resort to the proper strategies of manipulation. It becomes a bare *technique*.

Indeed, Herbert Hendin in his brilliant psychiatric analysis of the recent youth culture, *The Age of Sensation*, has pointed out how the imperatives of technology have been applied to the control of private emotion. Ironically, Hendin tells us, a culture which has succeeded in numbing genuine feeling and interpersonal warmth has latched onto various ploys for engineering and managing the "inner life." "Sensation is king in a nation in which it seems the best antidote to pleasurelessness and deadness." Ectasy as a consummation of programmed sensation becomes the new print-out for the biological and mental computers which are human beings themselves. And the computers cannot be shut off. "Once the most distinctive form of American envy was the desire for material possession," Hendin writes. "But now the most rapacious greed is for experience,"[8] experience of everything at once and nothing at all. Ecstasy becomes the style of robots. Soren Kierkegaard attacked his own age because it lacked "passion." Our age, having developed the wherewithal for modularizing and magnifying passion on a mass scale, has made the rare and truly passionate experience trivial. The electrification of our nerve endings becomes a routine sparking no genuine knowledge; and in that sense it has become the habit of a generation that is not prophetic but pathetic.

To make ecstasy a "style" of life requires, on the one hand, a preoccupation with the right equipment for personal fulfillment. One must take great pains to provide the correct blend of chanting, incense, or other forms of sensory excitation, not to mention congenial surroundings and plenty of free time. Furthermore, just as hedonism constitutes a complicated life plan for keeping pleasant sensations at a high pitch, so the pursuit of ecstacy entails vigilance in keeping the universe from losing its magical lustre or in tuning out the "bad vibrations." Dedication to a consistent stimulation of the senses is replaced by dependence on the permanent arousal of the "higher" centers of consciousness. The mania for consumption of material goods is pathetically echoed in the frenzied "purchase" of new methods for improving self-awareness, in the humming trade in instant nirvanas.

The relationship between *affluent* sensuality and the rage for ecstasy was brought home to me not too long ago in a conversation with a member of the International Society for Krishna Consciousness (ISKCON), one of the so-called Hare Krishna people. This young man, whom I shall call "Arjuna," related how he arrived at the "eternal happiness" of Krishna-consciousness. Arjuna told how, prior to his initiation, he had played in a rock band and indulged in the insouciant sensualism typical of the hip, music cenacles. He had tried a variety of hallucinogenic drugs, slept with a succession of women, flaunted fancy and expensive clothes. But such a carnival of the libido could not really satisfy him, Arjuna explained. His boundless appetites could not be met. So he finally turned to the teachings of Swami Prabhupada Bhaktivendanta, joined the band of saffron-robed disciples, and hit upon the immeasurable joy of Krishna-consciousness. He could always be "turned on" by reciting the mantra of "Hare Krishna," though one had to work at it. Hare Krishna devotees will tell you the numerous ways in which the "timeless pleasure" of the love of Krishna can be generated through dancing, eating delicately spiced foods, reading the *Bhagavad-Gita*, or simply chanting mantras. As Bhaktivedanta himself writes, "The joys of religiousness, economic development, sense gratification and liberation follow the devotional service of the Lord. In other words, a pure devotee does not lack any kind of happiness derived from any source."[9]

The theology of the Krishna society stresses the control of "gross" sensuality. The psychology of "getting high" on Krishna involves a kind of sublimated sensualism which draws its power from living in a setting of constant sensory agitation: brilliant colors, the hypnotic cadence of tambourines and flutes, tempting sweetmeats at the table. Every experience becomes charged with "pleasure," Arjuna said. One realizes that devotion is like forever drinking a heavenly "nectar." The Hare Krishna people have discovered the sacred of mastering sensuality in a fashion commensurated with traditional religious discipline. Individualism is suppressed; hence their communities are not beset with the dissension that has destroyed so many recent experiments in "free" communal living. The same attitudes and aims, when adopted selectively by the average person in his own home instead of in the temple, can lead to trouble. Ecstasy can become a savory addiction which saps the energies for dealing creatively with the challenges of daily living.

The regimentation of certain religious cults like the Hare Krishna people incorporates into the pursuit of ecstasy the necessity of work. Group survival is perceived as a value which cannot be ignored. ISKCON in the past few years has moved away from the character of sectarian freaks whose overt function is to amuse crowds in the street and to celebrate their own purified awareness. The industry of manufacturing incense, from which has come much of their livelihood, has been augments by the establishment of collective farms where crops are raised and a self-sufficient economy for the community is undertaken. A recent issue of *Back to Godhead*, the official magazine of ISKCON, pointed to the current economic crisis and the need to respond to it. Social realism has apparently captured the day. Scarcity assumptions are now part of the official creed.

The end of affluence raises afresh the issue of whether work and communal co-operation are more urgent life objectives than programmed felicity. At least the question remains as to whether the latter can be prudently prosecuted at the expense of the former. The fading of the so-called spiritual "explosion" of the past ten years may not signal a return to the waning values of the affluent society so much as new appreciation of human limitations and possibilities. Dionysian sexuality is still practiced in certain religious quarters; Esalen still is big business in California; followers of the Guru Maharaji are

still getting "blissed out" on the seductive "knowledge" which
he offers. Yet hard times may have diverted the middle classes
from such pastimes and left the sophisticated business of getting high to the corporate vice-presidents and the debutantes
from Shaker Heights. College students, who just a few years
ago spent the time out of the classroom smoking dope and mooning
over Baba Ram Dass, are now working as clerks and waitresses to
support themselves. The new rules for the pursuit of happiness
will require turning down the ecstatic and seeking to establish
a policy for living, not to mention a religious sensitivity,
which incorporates toil and routine. It may soon be evident
that sustained ecstasy is a luxury, like a new car every two
years, only the favored few can afford.

The Limits of Self-realization

The style of ecstasy is predicated on a certain valuation
of what human beings ought to strive for -- maximum intensity
of awareness, optimal development of personal talents. The
pursuit of ecstasy, therefore, absorbs the morality of the
human potential movement. "Allowing persons to die without
developing their full potentialities is at least as bad as
our current waste of natural resources,"[10] Seifert avers.
The analogy, nevertheless, may not be as persuasive as it
sounds. We must honestly ask ourselves whether the ideal of
self-realization can remain consistent when set over against
the problem of resources sufficient to preserve the lives and
happiness of individuals only in modest measure. The waste
of natural resources, in one crucial respect, is actually a
precondition to the cultivation of everyone's potential, since
the greatest possible enhancement of personal well-being means
in many cases that other goods, such as stewardship of the environment, must be sacrificed. The wasteful life-styles of

the affluent have not brought only mindless consumption and profligate spending. A certain degree of "waste" allows for the blossoming of individual aptitudes. If I have the convenience of a car to speed me to work every morning, instead of taking the bus, I have more time to read a book, meditate, or chat with my spouse. If I own an automatic dishwasher or an electric freezer, I can be writing a book instead of spending an hour scouring pans or shopping in the supermarket, none of which would be conducive to expanding my potential. On the other hand, there are those who endeavor to realize the "potential" of the grass in the yard by nurturing stunningly green lawns. From the ecological standpoint the liberal use of water and fertilizer is a "waste" of resources that could otherwise be employed in more socially advantageous ways.

With respect to the distribution of wealth in a society, moreover, it is apparent that those who have access to the amenities of life and who consume the greatest amount of resources are more likely to have the opportunity to dally with "experience." Psychotherapy, for instance, can cost as much as a new car. Unless resources are infinite, the personal freedoms enjoyed by one class of individuals encroaches on the freedoms of another class. A British noblewoman commented recently that one person's liberation requires the servitude of another. She recounted how she refused to have hired help merely so she could shore up the quality of her own life.

From a global vantage point the spread of affluence in this country, which has made possible the remaking of the old values of self-denial and hard work into the new morality of self-development, has been possible by our hogging of the natural and financial resources of the rest of the world. It has become a truism of late that even though we are such a small percentage of the earth's population we exploit the bulk of its wealth. No wonder the Third World countries are clamoring for a larger take. This situation makes understandable why the ethic of self-realization, prized in the Western nations, can have little meaning for an African peasant worried about the threat of famine, or for the government of a Latin American country bent upon land reform. The equable allocation of the means of existence takes precedence over maximizing the happiness of any given individual. Though we decry these attitudes as the seeds of a gray collectivism, they ultimately make sense in light of social conditions. Indeed, as economic growth tapers off in the United States and the problem of fairly distributing wealth becomes more acute, the choice between granting individual claims to self-enrichment and taking away from some to give to others will not be as easy as in the past. In the past the solution has always been to give more to everybody. The chief moral issue will not be how to actualize everyone's potential, but to support individual happiness without brutal coercion. Heilbroner rues the imminent danger of dictatorships which will "force" the people "to be free," to employ Rousseau's phrase. A more humane, but historically difficult solution, is the evolution of new social and religious values as part of an encompassing tradition where desires will be restrained, and individuals must find happiness in co-operative undertakings and service to others.

Unfortunately, the claim that individuals must sacrifice their potentials for the sake of social harmony is likely to offend many as some kind of new Puritanism, or at best a sophisticated pessimism. Ingrained habits of thinking die hard, and it is not difficult to think that we must choose between either an old-fashioned morality of self-abnegation or a new ethic of self-fulfillment. The dichotomy, however, is a false one. Any ethic which makes self-realization the goal of life winds up incomplete since the problem of reconciling competing claims to happiness is discounted. As the philosopher Immanuel Kant noted, happiness in itself is an elusive quarry. There can be no set standard for any particular individual as to what it actually takes truly to be happy. Man is the creature whose wants multiply endlessly, including the so-called "higher" wants. An ethic founded on the pursuit of happiness alone becomes an endless treadmill of satisfying elusive wants.

The same is true for an ethic of self-realization. The self is an infinite potential which can never be realized absolutely. The more one makes self-realization a passion, the more other obligations and values are discarded. John Dewey has remarked that whoever is absorbed only in realizing himself will, without fail, end up becoming totally self-centered. It is slowly becoming clear that the pop therapist, who bores into contemporary homo sapiens' psychic discontents promising a joyride of peak experiences to alleviate them, is scarcely different from the Madison Avenue advertiser who seeks to market new products by making the housewife fret whether her children's underwear is "whiter than white."

A resolution of the dilemma rests on finding a stable set of cultural norms and social duties in which happiness can be attained by satisfying one's role and living creatively in response to the needs and expectations of others. The self can be posited anew as primarily a social self rather than the sheaf of vague existential choices implied by the theory of self-realization. The good life can be redescribed as a style of participation in a web of social and familial ties lending a genuine "spiritual" magnitude to our workday activities. The irony is that we can be happy only when we stop trying so hard to be happy. We can only be happy when freedom entails reciprocity and accountability. We can rest only when there is a place to rest. Again in the words of Philip Slater the most "radical change" is "only the reinstatement of stability itself."[11]

Toward the Steady State

Renewed stability may, in fact, be unavoidable because of the very pressure toward a less volatile chemistry of human relationships within the new environment itself. We have discussed how the persistence of affluence conditions people not only to picture their world as inconstant but also to behave in ways which accelerate social fission and drift. The futurologist's projections of a twenty-first century in which the human mindscape dissolves into an auditorium of blinking strobe lights can turn out to be a self-fulfilling prophecy. The cult of happiness passes from a rational regard for an orderly dispensation of intellectual, civil, and material blessings, as it was in the thought of Jefferson and his contemporaries, to the philosophy of *carpe diem*, squeezing from the moment the elixir of ecstasy. The World is a whirling carousel. Let us eat, drink and have transcendental insight, for tomorrow we may let slip our opportunities.

But the true opportunity we are inclined to miss is that of striking an ecological balance between the claims of the self and the harmony of all potentialities in nature. Heretofore, "ecology" has, more or less, amounted to rescuing whales from extinction, or capping the chimneys of steel mills in Minnesota. It has implied a mystical feeling about the sanctity of what is left of the pre-technological phase of our planet's history. The interface existing between economics and ecology has only very recently been taken seriously. Economics was once thought to be the science of material growth, ecology its conscience. The coming age of scarcity will demand a marriage of economics with the advocacy of economic restraint. The "eco" in both "economics" and "ecology" comes from the same Greek root -- from "oiko-," meaning "house" or "household." It is the same root from which we derive "ecumenical," a word suggesting fraternal dialogue and the recognition of interdependence -- the connectedness of all beings who live "under the same roof." Economics and ecology merge into a new method or world view that we could call "ecotics." Ecotics would be the "science" of the pursuit of human happiness, not in the sense of rules for individual perfection, but in the sense of discovering principles of social and biological concord. If scarcity thwarts the goals of abundance for all, ecumenics would aim to show how scarce resources can be husbanded without social well-being languishing. If the human psyche ultimately proves unable to adapt to Toffler's helter-skelter world of tomorrow, ecotics would seek alternatives to mere adaptation; it would call for the creation of a new world. Ecotics would be the science of happiness; it would plot the best routes for achieving universal felicity within circumstances that seem to bar the fruition of many deep-rooted aspirations or to deny conventional expectations. We are not talking here of a disguised utilitarianism, a theory of the greatest happiness for the greatest number of people. The point is not to maximize happiness according to the old manuals; it is to rediscover and to re-educate with respect to what it takes to be happy. Ecotics would elevate organic relationships over individualism, contentment over striving, endurance over flux. It would represent, in a word, a new science of value.

Physicists, economists, and polotical scientists these days have introduced the expression, "steady-state," into our lexicon. The steady-state society is seen as a necessary epilogue to the story of affluence and constitutes the heart of ecotical planning. John Stuart Mill forecast the steady-state society as far back as the nineteenth century. He foresaw the eventual slowing of capitalism's expansion, which would carry with it a new stimulus toward "improving the Art of living."[12] The steady-state society emerges as the most practical alternative to be entertained by both visionaries and hard-boiled planners in considering the effects of curtailments in the economy on the working and leisure arrangements of ordinary people's lives. According to A. Daniel Burhans, a political scientist, the hallmark of the steady-state society.

> is the maintenance of a constant stock of people and physical wealth, or capital. Steady-state is not equivalent to stagnation. The steady-state society is open and creative. Stocks do not of themselves remain constant; people die; wealth is physically consumed, worn out, depreciated, replaced. But in a steady-state society, inflow (i.e., birth and production) is carefully and methodically regulated by outflow (death and consumption).[13]

A purely abstract, economic model of the steady-state is relatively simple to construct. The rate of "flow" of goods and services, which we discussed in Chapter 1, or what Burhans calls "throughput," is slowed. The paramount value is not to fuel "growth," which involves waste and the overutilization of vital resources such as petroleum, but to obtain the highest quality of life from the lowest production levels and the greatest enjoyment of what is available. As Burhans explains: "A low rate of throughput for the stock of wealth...means low production and equally low consumption."[14] Furthermore, "in order to slow down throughput, the durability of goods must be maximized and/or other goods must be recycled."[15]

On the other hand, anticipation of the steady-state has even vaster implications for the future of Western culture. With present population trends, the outlook is for a more uniform reserve of people in society. A lower birth rate and increasing longevity augurs plainly that the same faces will be around longer. By the same token, the age distribution of the populace will be gradually skewed toward the older sector. The idolatry of the young present in Western society for numerous generations will fade because of the sheer demographic decline of people in that age bracket. Add to this state of affairs a shrinking of the base of wealth and a new culture will most likely appear. Aging makes people more settled in their ways. We used to consider this tendency part of the curse of growing old. It may be reappreciated as an advantage. Settling down reinforces the values of permanence. The expension of the life span may make the relentless pursuit of new techniques of happiness seem futile, if not gratuitous. Studies on the mentality of the old have indicated that long years tend to truncate what were once insatiable youthful drives and wants as well as to bring about a kind of spiritual delight in the simpler attractions of the world, such as a poinsetta at Christmas or a child romping in the afternoon sun.[16] Such a quiescence of the soul, a reining in of our hereditary Faustian impulses, may be much more "functional" for the steady-state than any of the chic life philosophies of recent vintage.

Reduced throughput in the economic sphere leads to a less active and checkered life for people at the grass roots. The pace of living itself slackens, and common perceptions about what is ultimately real and estimable are altered. The worth of enduring customs and institutions are rediscovered, just as cheap, short-lived and shoddily manufactured items are now rejected in favor of the sturdy and well designed. In the steady-state society, people will probably hop less from one intellectual fad to another, or revolve less through a series of personal identity crises in the life cycle. Similarly they will not sell their homes and buy new ones every eighteen months, or go through spouses and lovers with an abandon otherwise reserved for fine pipes and wines. The forced economy of resourcefulness exemplified in the old New England jingle, "Use it up/wear it out/make it do/or do without," will serve to re-stitch the entire fabric of daily experience. We will learn again to enjoy the imperishable. The old calculus of frequent and vivid sensations, of repeated "charges" in the circuits of experience, will give way to a reappraisal of how little it actually takes from the *qualitative* standpoint to ensure contentment. Consider the young person who "fills" his Sunday afternoon by listening to a stack of records on his stereo or watching a baseball triple header, or of the parent who takes a stroll with his pre-school daughter to the park, drinking in the sunny moments while she plays and giggles, relishing the simplicity of it all without boredom.

We have been inundated lately with clichés concerning the changes in society which the end of affluence will usher in. Our infatuation with the automobile will have to be toned down; we will grow and eat more of our own carrots or spinach instead of relying on the pre-packaged variety; we will have more old-style "togetherness" in family affairs. For the most part these virtually innocuous prophecies may prove to be little more than wishful thinking. So far we have steered clear of outright predictions because of the complexity and precariousness of the historical process itself. We can only register trends and make what would seem to be reasonable surmises.

On the other side, there are the Jeremiahs who envision something like a plunge into a new dark age -- the revival of Thomas Hobbes' picture of the "war of all against all" in the state of nature. Robert Vacca's *The Coming New Dark Age* (Doubleday, 1974), is in this mood. A more plausible, but equally disheartening work, is Paul Ehrlich's *The End of Affluence* (Ballantine, 1974). Ehrlich soberly envisages the coming collapse of the world monetary system, the spread of political anarchy, and a fierce rivalry not only among nations but also among individuals for the dwindling necessities of life. Ehrlich expects people to begin exhibiting bomb-shelter behavior -- hoarding supplies and fending off intruders -- even though the disasters will have nothing to do with "the bomb." He counsels everyone to prepare for doomsday by stockpiling gold, building up food caches, and buying a gun. If the Ehrlich brand of prophecy is correct, the end of affluence is a grisly horror to contemplate, and the notion of a gradual refinement of human existence appears pollyanish.

Fortunately, Ehrlich can be dismissed as the type of writer who stays in the public limelight by virtue of his scary scenarios for the future. *The End of Affluence* thus rehashes the slick apocalypticism of *The Population Bomb*, his earlier best-seller. The problem with Ehrlich's premonition of life in the bunker is that it fails to take into account the historical fact that anarchy never continues for long, that new social configurations and institutions emerge in order to adjust to new conditions. Indeed, Ehrlich's advice that we all gird ourselves for a siege against our very life, limb, and property smacks of a cynicism which, were his recommendations taken seriously, would inflame the social tensions bound to smoulder over the next few decades. The steady-state society is a more realistic prospect, even though it may take much turmoil and psychic re-attuning before we get there. Whether the rules of conduct in the steady-state society are dragooned upon us by repressive government or observed naturally because of a fundamental change in cultural values is, of course, a matter of how well and fast people come to understand and react to the new situation.

If history provides any lesson, however, it is principally that the situation will change more rapidly than people can comprehend. But that does not guarantee some irreversible calamity. It means only that a new culture, with its moral traditions, will *have* to grow upon the bones of the old. Such a culture may not suit all the specifications which we would want. As Slater has remarked in his most recent book, "Cultures cannot be planned, nor are they very logical. They need only be coherent."[17] The suggestion here is not that mankind will somehow "muddle through," but that social holism invariably take precedence over empty individualism. And since that is the case, the expectation can be that the post-affluent world will find its own equilibrium, or what we have called the steady-state. The flaw in Ehrlich's vision is not merely that it is painted black on black. The difficulty is that his vison depends on the present instead of the future. Just as Hobbes unwittingly patterned his tooth-and-claw picture of the state of nature on the political tempests of his day, so Ehrlich reads the future through his perception of the competitive individualism and avarice of the affluent society of the past. The state of nature, even when drawn in Ehrlich's sophisticated fashion, must still be consigned to fiction. There is yet no evidence that historical fiction is about to become history itself.

The Allotment of Sparse Wealth and the "New" Morality

If in the future the guidelines for happiness must be written around the limitations of life in the steady-state society, the ethical and political formulas of the past will have to be revised also. In the affluent society morality is personal and politics a contest of special interest groups. Superabundance yields no incentive to create or sustain community, except in the purely nostalgic or rarefied emotional sense that Haight-Ashbury and Woodstock embodied for the counterculture. The result is that there exists no social lever for moral choices. The narcissism of individuals cut off from common experiences and concerns leads to the illusion of autarchy in the ethical sphere. Everyone chases his own rainbow, tags after his own fantasies, and accedes to his unconscious urges.

Politically, the concept of "nation" in either the integral or pluralistic sense collapses into random modes of identification. The well-to-do, excluded psychically from the larger

community because of their immense privilege, are prone to
indulge themselves in reactionary myths about a libertarian
society (the H. L. Hunt syndrome), or to swing the other way
and imagine themselves to be outlaws and champions of the
oppressed "masses" whom they have never really known or understood (as in the Patty Hearst episode). While the very rich
are culling extremist ideologies, the middle classes tend to
shirk commitments to any movement and adopt a "what's in it
for me?" attitude. Labor unions, for example, lose their
proletarian fervor and begin catering to the status quo. The
feeling of brotherhood in dedication to a cause disappears, and
patriotism tends to become venal and superficial. When a number
of hardhats were interviewed in 1970 and asked about the motives
for their spirited defense of their nation and its president,
their response was that only in this land could they reap such
a high standard of living. The old shibboleths about having
only one life to give to the country were tellingly absent. In
the legislative realm, the practice of doing politics to meet
selfish interests, rather than to live up to some national
ideals, has been behind years of graft, corruption, boondoggles,
and fiscal waste. But such vices could easily be tolerated in
the affluent society. There was no overwhelming societal
pressure to eliminate them. Who could care if a particular
interest group is slyly extorting public money provided the
average citizen's paycheck keeps up with or rises faster than
the cost of living?

But when the so-called "economic pie" shrinks appreciably
and competition for a restricted share of the national wealth
becomes more marked, as is happening now, a renewed concern
for social equity and the good of the public as a whole will
be more likely. At first, the natural tendency may be the
opposite. Power elites and people in favored positions may
struggle to maintain their past prerogatives. Thus, while

the average purchasing power of the American worker has been declining since 1973, certain kinds of professionals, such as doctors and corporation executives, have held their own -- in some instances, even improved their status. The self-congratulatory phrase, "I'm alright, Jack, I've got mine," may be said more stridently by those who have the clout to uphold privilege. Among those who cannot boast of power and privilege the reaction, in comparison, will probably be resentment as well as agitation to punish the more conspicuous custodians of wealth. The outrage against the oil companies in this country is an obvious sign of such a reaction. Yet scapegoating and "soak the rich" campaigns, such as Huey Long's plan over a generation ago to help most everybody while garroting a few select millionaires, will ultimately prove futile. The desire for equity must be transformed into deflation of the aims of all but the truly underprivileged in society. As Andrew Hacker has shown, the venerable belief in the existence of a "ruling class" which perpetually skims off most of the cream of the GNP needs re-examination. Neither the bulk of capital nor the major percentage of personal income in this country is in the hands of a tiny number of distinct individuals. Rather, capital is largely controlled by boards of directors, such as business executives, or minor entrepreneurs whom we would ordinarily consider "middle class."

Hacker concludes that "blaming 'the rich' or a 'ruling class' no longer makes much sense."[18] If the answer to scarcity is a reallotment of wealth, it will affect many people who probably do not expect to be affected. Moreover, any significant diminution of the total available wealth will make it necessary to take something out of the pockets of both ordinary wage earners and the titans of corporate finance. The real issue will be how much to take from whom, and what is the minimal decent standard of living that should be assured for all. The "rich" will have to make weighty sacrifices, but in doing so

they will not be alone. In order to avoid, however, the easy
recriminations which might be directed by one group at another,
new standards must be based on rudimentary moral assumptions
about who deserves what and for what reasons. The disposition
of certain groups to telescope their own private advantage into
the public interest ("what's good for General Motors is good
for the country") must give place to policies and a consensus
of principles encompassing the larger picture. Ethically
speaking, the maxim of promoting everyone's personal happiness
to the hilt must be supplanted with the goal of meting out
scarce opportunities for "happiness" in the old sense so that
new expectations about what happiness really means can grow.

The "new" morality necessary to advance justice in the
steady-state society, though, cannot be simply old-fashioned
altruism. Nor can it be some doctrine of personal asceticism.
Both altruistic and ascetic moralities have their origin in
the ethics of individualism. The altruist is supposed to give
a portion of his bounty, perhaps after he has gratified himself without undue excess, to others who are in need. He is
motivated by some diffuse "fellow-feeling" rather than an authentic sense of his own position of interdependence and responsibility. In its aristocratic form, altruism becomes the
principle of *noblesse oblige*, the duty of the person of high
station to show regard for the less fortunate without really
compromising his own privilege. The legacy of philanthropy in
America fits such a model. The philanthropist could be a robber
baron and have a good conscience in the same breath. In our
contemporary democratic era, the liberal professional classes,
who have seen fit to aggrandize themselves as much as possible
while still "helping out" the unemployed and slum mothers, are
less evident examples.[19] On the other hand, the welfare system,
by keeping people at subsistence level without allowing them
opportunities to participate with dignity in middle-class social
life, illustrates the bankrupt logic of altruism as public policy.

Ascetic morality is cut from much the same bark. The ascetic willfully denies himself happiness so that others may benefit, either tangibly or by example, from his austerity. Asceticism, however, is usually reserved for saints and revolutionaries who pit themselves against oppression and seek to inspire trust in their leadership. Only the man of historical destiny can be a true ascetic. Asceticism as a social morality is something of a contradiction; to deny oneself happiness for the sake of another's happiness cannot be a universal value scheme when the objective is happiness overall. Furthermore, the everyday psychology of asceticism, as Luther learned in his monastery, tends to breed selfishness more than charity. The rigid ascetic becomes preoccupied with quelling his own appetites; hence he closes off the possibility of true generosity and a community spirit. In communist Russia ascetic morality has been melded with social materialism, with the result lack of productivity among workers. They yearn for the comfortable life but balk at having to labor in a soulless and regimented society which cynically denies them promised satisfactions. Similarly, the asceticism of the "Protestant work ethic" in America has been bound up with an economy producing more than enough material goods to make people happy; yet people do not turn out to be happy. The ascetic sacrifices his happiness now in order, perhaps, to achieve happiness of some kind later. But the ascetic plies, after all, the art only of being dissatisfied. To give up things in a sincere manner requires that we do not genuinely need or want the things we give up.

But how can a whole society be made to settle for less? How can desires blown up to grotesque proportions throughout the generations, and needs artificially contrived in the consumer society, be reduced to essentials? How can the passion for the repeadedly new and titillating be quieted? Human beings cannot be forced to settle for less. The auguries now in the world-press that we will have to lower our personal expectations are hardly encouraging to those who have been instructed all their lives to expect more and more. Hence, come the deeprooted and desperate apathy of our age. Although government austerity programs may repair the economic breaches that will increasingly open, they will not salve the psychic and spiritual wounds. Nor can we rely on some inborn "moral sense" to magically revive when the new situation becomes intelligible to most persons. Morality is a product of culture and tradition. The revamping of culture and tradition will take years at best. Nonetheless, it is at this sensitive point that hope is born. Culture and tradition, as we have seen, ultimately spring from religion, from revelation, from a disclosure to man as to why the world appears as it does. In the next chapter we investigate the possibilities for a religion to forge the "new personality" who can live happily in the post-affluent order.

NOTES TO CHAPTER 6

1. Thomas Jefferson, *Writings*, XVI, 118. Quoted in Howard M. Jones, *The Pursuit of Happiness* (Cambridge: Harvard University Press, 1953), p. 15.

2. cf. David Potter, *People of Plenty* (Chicago: University of Chicago Press, 1954).

3. Theodore Roszak, *Where the Wasteland Ends* (Garden City, NY: Doubleday & Co., 1973), cf. Chapters 10 & 11.

4. Harvey Seifert, *Reality and Ecstasy* (Philadelphia: The Westminster Press, 1974), p. 90.

5. Seifert, p. 87.

6. Alan Watts, *Beyond Theology* (New York: Random House, 1964), p. 41.

7. Philip Slater, *The Pursuit of Loneliness* (Boston: Beacon Press, 1970), p. 139.

8. Herbert Hendin, *The Age of Sensation* (New York: W. W. Norton, 1975).

9. A. C. Bhaktivedanta Swami Prabhupada, *The Nectar of Devotion* (New York: Bhaktivedanta Book Trust, 1970), p. 13.

10. Seifert, *op. cit.*, p. 84.

11. Slater, *op. cit.*, p. 128.

12. J. S. Mill, *Principles of Political Economy* (London: Longmans, Green, and Co., 1929), p. 751.

13. A. D. Burhans, "The Steady State," *The Center Magazine* (Jan./Feb. 1975), p. 19.

14. Burhans, p. 22.

15. *ibid.*

16. See here an article by David Gutman, "The Premature Gerontocracy: Themes of Aging and Death in the Youth Culture," in Arien Mack (ed.), *Death in American Experience* (New York: Shocken Books, 1973), pp. 50-82.

17. Philip Slater, *Earthwalk* (Garden City, NY: Doubleday & Co., 1974), p. 219.

18. Andrew Hacker, "What Rules America?" *New York Review of Books* (May 1, 1975), p. 13.

19. There seems to be mounting evidence that the "Great Society Programs" launched in the 1960's actually put more money into the pockets of the social workers and welfare administrators than into the bank accounts of the poor, who were supposed to benefit from the largesse of the government.

CHAPTER 7

The Transfiguration of Tradition: A Religion
of the Obvious, Simple, Appropriate,
and Natural

"Simplify, simplify."
-- Henry David Thoreau

Truth is the Obvious

Once upon a time an unlettered neighborhood handyman engaged me in an impromptu discussion of the nature of "truth." After I had given a long-winded and properly qualified exposition of my own point of view, he caught me by surprise with an ingenuous remark. "You know," he drawled, "you just answered my question. You just told me that truth is the obvious." How simple-minded and out-of-sorts that formulation seemed at the time! Yet my refusal to acknowledge any significance in his statement was probably due more to my youthful *hauteur* and pseudo-sophistication than to any genuine philosophical acumen. Indeed, the force of such a proposition must unfailingly grate upon the tastes of modern intellectuals, including myself. From grammar school onward, our entire educational system teaches us to be vigilantly critical and reserved with regard to pithy generalities like the handyman's. All opinions must be stated with certain ceremonial caveats and albeits -- "providing that"'s and "then again"'s. Intuitions are shelved if they cannot be extensively demonstrated by some other kind of truth-testing.

Defended with too much enthusiasm, they are likely to be dismissed as the stuff of fanaticism.

Some educators are belatedly coming to the recognition that this approach to the quest for insight and understanding may have outlived its usefulness. When dogmatism as well as religious and social superstitions presented a formidable threat to mature inquiry and humane morality, the procedure of relentless clarification and criticism was justified. Yet in an age when most traditional values and beliefs have been summarily exterminated, the procedure becomes otiose. At worst, it breeds nihilism. Privatized ethics and narcissism in religion and psychology are larger cultural responses to the total loss of evident criteria of what is real. As a matter of style, such a massive assault on the average person's trust in his own intuitions (we might say "common sense) eventuates in the creation of two primary types of "knower" in society, both unlike our handyman: the pedant or the pettifogger who has to gloss every simple observation with technical bombast or erudite quibbles, *and* the garden variety mystic who comprehends the "all" in a flash and therefore cannot speak plainly either. "Those who say do not know and those who know do not say," observed Lao-Tzu. Truth is no longer the obvious but the obscure.

The meaning of the term "obvious," however, may not be itself that obvious. Etymology tells us that the root connotation of the term is "standing in the way of." Something that stands in the way supposedly cannot be missed. An obvious piece of evidence lies "right before our eyes." Yet invariably we perceive selectively, and what is directly in front of us or in our way tends to be overlooked. We have arrived at a culture in which the obvious chronically goes unnoticed. For some perverse reason we have become like Balaam in the Biblical story. Not seeing what his ass saw, that his path was blocked by an angel of God, he pummelled the ass to go forward even though the dumb beast was more attuned to his immediate surroundings than the prophet himself. The Biblical tale concludes with Balaam finally discerning the obvious: "Then Yahweh opened the eyes of Balaam and he saw the angel of Yahweh standing in the way." (Numbers 22:31) To apprehend the obvious took a kind of enlightenment on Balaam's part which was at the same time a divine epiphany. For us in modern culture the obvious may not be obvious at all. We do not sense the presence of the angel. And in this respect truth remains fogged by our prejudices and inattention.

It may well be that we do not perceive the obvious truths and values of life because we have grown bored. Affluence has given rise to a style of boredom which mirrors the dull restlessness of the homeless mind. The mentality of constant consumption and endless self-development impairs the elementary enjoyments of what is familiar and close at hand. We take pleasure only in the thoroughly novel, unexplored, or outlandish. Our glut of personal possessions produces a surfeit of sensations and experiences leading us to devalue all possessions, sensations, and experiences. We cannot accept our world for what it is because we are hell-bent always on uncovering new worlds. Just as the child swamped with toys tends to be careless of them, so the person caught up in the whirl of experience learns not to give much credence to anything that really happens to him.

As a college professor who reads books all the time, I must confess that I have acquired the regrettable habit of never going through any of them with careful attention. The toil and discipline of writing a book in one's own words thus becomes a necessary therapy. The typical young couple today who absorbs the peer ideology that since all relationships are temporary, a succession of mates will probably "broaden your horizons," finds it easy to avoid struggling to know each other in any authentic depth. In this respect it could be advantageous for our society to revive the custom of marrying one's childhood sweetheart. The simple and obvious are no longer merely taken for granted; they are *condemned*. How often do we find ourselves snickering at the old man who rides the same noon-hour bus everyday and chats with the passengers, the rural Kansas lady who can tell you about every road and farmhouse in her county, the little boy who wants to pause at the park each day to watch the squirrels scamper up and down the trees?

One day my wife asked me if I wanted to take a walk around the neighborhood with her and our little son. I replied that I did not because I had seen what there was to see in the neighborhood too many times. She asked me what I had seen, and curiously I could not remember. The next time I strolled through the neighborhood I realized that I had, in truth, been aware of very little. By habit I had ignored the simple and obvious. I was instinctively bored with a set of experiences that I had never really had in the first place.

Tradition and Simplicity

The simplifying of life and experience together enables a person to achieve a harmony with his world and at the same time fill out his own vision. The commonplace features of one's environment heretofore merely smudges on a lusterless landscape become glowing markers. What formerly were dull throbs of sensation are transformed into "divine" manifestations, into veritable epiphanies. What is obscure in our midst becomes obvious for the first time. The revaluation of the plain and everyday, however, can come about only with a shift in the expectations of people as to what is relevant or engages them. Affluence, and its unsettled, allegro tempo of experience, encourage us unfortunately not to drink from innumerable freshets of meaning that trickle at any moment from our environment. We are trained to monitor not the subtle but the gross, not the slow growing but the fast maturing; to trade the enduring appreciation for the cheap thrill; to delight in the appearance rather than in the essences of things. Tennyson's flower in the crannied wall is only a flower, and probably a plastic one at that. Affluence has introduced what René Guenon has termed the "reign of quantity" into the life worlds of the human masses. But the reign of quantity does not entail precisely what Guenon suggested: the ascendancy of scientific method and statistical models in the arbitration of questions of truth or value. The reign of quantity is a pathology of the affluent society which substitutes for permanent, qualitative meanings a mania for seriality and intensity. This disorder affects not only the engineers and bureaucrats, but also the gurus and seers of the new wave of "spirituality." Whoever requires from instant to instant a surge of energy that will arouse the hypothalamus can appreciate nothing except the sensations1. But the sensational by definition is the peak, not the slopes of the mountain; and many more wild blooms are to be found on the mountainside than on the bleak and craggy summit.

Restoration of simplicity and surety in both our inward sensing and our outward deportment depends, as we have indicated, on a place for traditional channels of human intercourse. Living traditions are gyroscopes which steady the evolution of morals and institutions. To attack traditions in an era of generalized anomie is like the discredited medical practice of bleeding the infirm in order to cure them. Yet traditions perform a role more important than any conserving function. Traditions serve to simplify the range of possible experiences in a culture, and thereby free the mind to refresh itself from a vital source of meaning. Traditions lend shape and content to the familiar

data of the world, disclosing the obvious without making it
trivial. The trivialization of experience, paradoxically, proceeds only when the mind cannot rest content with any state of
consciousness, with any insight, it has attained. Today's
breakthroughs become tomorrow's clichés. But a culture which
cannot accept any breakthrough as truly significant or lasting
winds up making all experience a colossal cliché. What was once
taken for self-expression and creativity sinks into apathy and
cynicism, just as nineteenth century Romanticism petered out
into decadence and nihilism. It has become an old bromide in
the history of the arts that genuine creation and innovation
must have a tradition in which to innovate. The poverty of
modernism in painting and poetry has been ascribed to the lack
of any coherent canons of art. Having violated and discarded
all esthetic norms, modernism has nothing left to revolt against,
as Philip Toynbee has so elequently pointed out.[1] Similarly,
an almost comic sign of this malaise is the fact that "creativity" itself has become a hackneyed concept. Recently, I
discovered a manufacturer who turns out children's tee-shirts
and duffle bags with "creative" conspicuously stencilled across
them. If creativity can be conjured up by machine lettering
then it has ceased by its very nature to be creativity at all.

Historically, the handmaidens of creative adaptation within
a tradition have been myth and ritual. Myths are paradigmatic
stories told and retold within a special setting to give substance to everyday experiences. The experiences themselves are
measured, however, against the experiences, not the other way
around. Indeed, the myth informs the experience. The Christian
myth of the resurrection for hundreds of years provided cues
for the empirical judgments of historians, artists, and theolotians, as well as for those of the common people. The *imitatio
Christi* was the martyrs, and penitents have taken the cricified
Lord as an exemplar. Myths are recurring "revelations," insofar

as they function as a set of master symbols through which the underlying significance of human life is continuously expressed. Mircea Eliade, in fact, has shown that the myth is the quintessential key to "reality" for traditional peoples. Apart from the myth, ordinary experience has no gravity or purpose; it is like a wedding without vows, a band tuning up without ever playing music.

Rituals, by the same token, are traditional patterns of behavior conforming to the mythical prototype. The rite is not an empty gesture or formalism, as we have come to think of it today. Such an attitude can develop only when the meaning of both the myth and the ritual is sapped. On the contrary, the rite embodies the mythical view of the world. The performer of the rite acts out or dramatizes the myth so that it moves from tale to the semblance of actual events. The Navajo Indian, for example, who carries out the healing ritual of the sand-painting, is self-consciously enacting the myth of the creation of the universe; he is aligning his own mortal gestures with the felt rhythm of the cosmos. The word "ritual" is etymologically akin to the Sanskrit term *rita*, which can be rendered loosely as the "order" of life itself. Myth, therefore, is not a patent fiction or falsity, a rude and savage belief; nor is it a rigid, ceremonial act smothering "free expression." Myth and ritual consist in living forms of communal cognition and behavior which ground our finite selves in a frame of universal reference.

Abandonment of myth and ritual has conventionally been blamed on some mysterious process called "enlightenment" or "secularization." Whereas it is true that the scientific world picture of modernity has left little room for the old myths and their supporting rites, it is not the case that such anchors of mythical experience have been hoisted up entirely. Contemporary myths arise in every generation, whether they be the science-fiction themes of UFO landings, so brilliantly analyzed by

Carl Jung, or the political myth of American national invulnerability. Similarly, rituals as stereotyped behaviors linger on in such vestigial forms as the singing of the national anthem before sporting events or the reciting of the Preamble of the Constitution on the Fourth of July. The popular pomp and pageantry surrounding the Bicentennial may be taken as a somewhat feeble and belated effort to invigorate ritually the myth of America's beginnnings.

The enervation of modern myth, however, has less to do with changing conceptions of reality than with the disappearance of a common pivot for social experience. If our need to survive as a people no longer seems relevant, and if individual preference or whim takes the place of shared values, then a well-defined and commonly accepted paradigm of experience is impossible. Genuine myth is not just a story, it is *our* story. In contemporary culture, though, all biographies are private, all stories are idiosyncratic and therefore unintelligible to others. Wider and compelling myths give way to personal wish-fulfillments and fantasies. The eccentric visionary becomes more interesting in literature, in philosophy, or in religion than the creative bearer of a traditional perspective. EST, a glossy, California-born mutation of the Human Potential Movement epitomizes this social attitude with its beguiling precept: "You are the author of your own universe."

The belief that a solitary individual can create his own universe, like the God of the Old Testament, *ex nihilo* ("out of nothing"), is an absurdity that only the disinherited modern imagination could countenance. Without vital, collective myths ritual action degenerates into spasmodic, undirected gyrations, as in contemporary dance fashions. All behavior, moral behavior included, is stripped of its bearings and becomes a frantic and exhausting search for gratification, like the rat in the psychology laboratory deprived of its food reward. The recovery of a stable order necessitates not only the rebirth of tradition in the abstract, but the building up of the dynamic elements of tradition. Myth and ritual furnish an experiential scaffolding for a culture dedicated to the maintenance of a genial and humane climate of life for all. But such a climate can only be preserved if the purpose of human existence is redescribed, not in terms of individual liberty and self-perfection, but according to norms which betoken how the person and the social organism converge within the ultimate scheme of things.

On Doing What is Appropriate

In a noteworthy address delivered at the American Academy of Religion meeting in 1972, the native American scholar and writer, Scott Mamaday, recounted the tale of an Indian man whose family had no food in the larder, yet who refused to go into the mountains to hunt for deer. His wife was pregnant at the time, and the man explained that it was not "appropriate" for him to take a life when he was "about to receive the gift of life."

Gauged by the yardstick of utilitarian morality, or even the ethics of personal advantage, the Indian man's act would seem queer -- "inappropriate." Yet the man's decision was guided by a more discriminate sensibility than mere self-interest. The mood of reverence for life -- the feeling that the events of birth and death compose a delicate equilibrium not to be upset -- *undergirds* a morality and a world vision that is *superior* to the paltry concerns of a singular existence. Doing what is "appropriate" in a situation is dictated by a holistic understanding of how the experiences of self and world fuse together. The refusal of the man was not motivated by some fugitive impluse; nor was it a "teleological suspension

of the ethical," such as Kierkegaard talked about -- the
repudiation of conventional or practical moral rules at the
behest of a "higher" calling or private intuition. It was
based on a traditional Indian apprehension of how man must
comport himself if the laws of the universe are not to be
violated. It reflected a "way" of knowing and doing that
suggested a profound grasp of the multitextured fabric of
life itself. Indian poetry in chanting and song evinces a
rich perception of how life traces complex, but obvious
patterns into which man must incorporate himself. Consider
the following chant of the Tewa:

>My words are tied in one
>With the great mountains,
>With the great rocks,
>With the great trees,
>In one with my body
>And with my heart.
>
>Do you all help me
>With supernatural power,
>And you, Day!
>And you, Night!
>All of you see me,
>One with this world![3]

Through the power of sacred language the Indian establishes the
appropriate connections between his own personality and the
workings of nature. His knowledge of what is real, not to
mention his very actions, are configured by an unshakable sense
of everything belonging to its own time or place.

Here we have the lesson of traditional societies: that the
good life does not hinge on the liberty of personal choice but
on learning appropriate responses to a world both suffered and
enjoyed. Such responses indicate a willingness of the person
to conform the agenda of his own life to the realistic possibilities which his world leaves open to him. But to conform
one's life to a higher order is not the same as mindless

conformity to a social system. Conformity has become a dirty word in the contemporary argot because it suggests strangling one's own spontaneity or originality to appease the arbitrary claims of the group. In a traditional society the principles of conduct and the rules for inferring what is appropriate or inappropriate need not be purely arbitrary. Instead, tradition is planted in the terra firma of common experience and collective memory. To make appropriate responses in the traditional manner is not to crush the personality; it is to strengthen it by giving one mastery over his own impulses in obedience to a universal, moral law. The seemingly quaint term, "virtue," implying adherence to such a law, has the root meaning of "strength" or "power." The virtuous man is not weakwilled, and anonymous, but powerful and a discrete personality. His power derives from his participation in the sacred procession of life, in his selection of appropriate roles and deeds.

Herbert Fingarette, for instance, has expounded such a view of human action of finely crafted ritual through his anatomy of Confucian philosophy. According to Fingarette, Confucius urged a renaissance of social decorum wherein private habits and intentions could be reshaped in concert with the idea of dignity. For Confucius, dignity was understood not merely in the sense of individual autonomy or social membership, but also in the sense of a unification of one's most psychic needs with the imperative of social order without traducing the limits placed by nature upon us all. Fingarette writes that Confucius commended "a life in which human conduct can be intelligible in natural terms and yet be attuned to the sacred, in which the practical, the intellectual and the spiritual are equally revered and harmonized in the one act -- the act of *li*."[4] The Chinese word *li* implies a complex harmony, pattern, and rhythm for all of life expressed through social custom and personal behavior. It is the process whereby the ideal character of a given individual is realized.

C. S. Lewis made a similar plea in his book *The Absolition of Man*. Lewis attacked the "innovator" who mercilessly assaults, as a matter of reflex if not of conscience, commonly cherished beliefs and traditional values simply because they are that way. The fruits of the innovator are incommensurably bitter, even though in his righteous fury to fell the rotting trunks of tradition he still hopes for a stump from which will burst new shoots. The tragedy of the innovator is that he wants to "make men without chests and expect of them virtue and enterprise."[5] The innovators are those who "laugh at honour and are shocked to find traitors in our midst."[6] In contrast to the iconoclastic way of the innovator, Lewis proposes an ethic which imitates the *Tao*, the "Way in which the universe goes on, the Way in which things everlastingly emerge, still and tranquilly, into space and time."[7] (Interestingly, Lewis infers his morality of the *Tao* from Confucian texts.) The implication of Lewis' argument is simply that moral and social activity cannot stand alone as self-supporting; they must be confirmed as a set of simple, obvious, and appropriate responses to life as it is undergone and interpreted. The degradation of culture and tradition poisons the natural forms of human existence; it "abolishes" the worth of man himself.

The difficulty, though, with Fingarette and Lewis is that much of their rhetoric smacks strongly of nostalgic *traditionalism*. The notion of "cosmic" order is quite slippery to grasp in an age of scientific cosmology and sociological relativism. If myth and ritual are meant to have a significant influence in the coming society, they cannot consist merely in the resuscitation of dead paradigms. It is only through make-believe that we can style ourselves as Confucian gentlemen steeped in the metaphysics of the China of twenty-five hundred years ago. Nor can we remake ourselves into Christian traditionalists in the fashion that Anglican conservatives such as T. S. Eliot and

Lewis have, perhaps obliquely, yearned for. New traditions must germinate out of new experiences, or at least out of recurring experiences that have an up-to-date character. The principle of appropriate response must be expressed through new structures of action and meaning. We must not pine for a bygone way of life with the innocence with which we watch sentimental sagas of midwestern pioneer families on television, or go back through music to the ragtime era.

James Sellers in *Warming Fires* has addressed himself to the problem of salvaging and resymbolizing community in a manner that will serve in lieu of traditional value and meaning systems. Sellers, like most thoughtful writers in this area, perceives well the catastrophic and depersonalizing aspects of our affluent, technological society. He does not give much credence to primitivists such as Roszak who want to dismantle just about all of contemporary civilization, or the new pietists among the encounter culture who are cock-sure that the salvation of society can be achieved simply by "getting in touch with your feelings" and by love alone. Sellers emphasizes the fact of interdependence which is increasingly becoming a conscious reality in our culture, and presses for a model of community which will take this situation into account. Such a community must institutionalize the now lapsed attitude of mutual caring -- the "brother's keeper" precept. "Interdependence and care are the clues to" the new identity of such a community.[8] Care and the recognition of interdependence, Sellers insists, will lead to a more healthy linkage between persons and institutions. Rather than letting federal bureaucracies, corporations, and bullying interest-groups toy with our destinies, we will take charge once more. For "from now on, we must make our institutions express the benefits of interdependence -- and not let them dominate us."[9] Our present society will, in short, be transformed not on the outside but on the inside. Its complexity will be preserved, but on the inside. Its complexity will be preserved, but preserved for the welfare of the populace in general instead of for big business and political power-brokers.

Altogether, however, Seller's stated wish to "light a new fire," as he puts it, is slightly specious. His homilies about the need for "care" recall vague memories of the pastors and theologians of the 1960's with their interminable platitudes about the necessity to react to the social injustices and uprisings of the period with "concern." Anyone who was not "concerned" courted the danger of being an unchristian lout. But concern is a rather sloppy category in ethics. Nor does it usually have much palpable effect. From 1966 to 1972 or thereafter the General Assembly of the United Presbyterian Church performed to small avail an annual ceremony of expressing its "concern" about the Vietnam War. "Care" may have more decided emotional impact, but it cannot create communities that outlive the first neighborly expressions of regard for one another.

Interdependence is a condition of life which the end of affluence should underscore to more and more of us, as Sellers seems to understand. With reference to the energy crisis and the decline of the automobile as the visible ensign of American society's obsession with property, independence, and status, Sellers notes: "By depending less on the props of technology we shall certainly be led to depend more on each other."[10] But this dependence can never by itself bind people together. A number of random studies at the darkest hour of the gasoline shortages in 1973 and 1974 revealed that when people, accustomed to insular lives, are willy-nilly thrown together, there is liable to be more friction than felicity. Families who had to stay home weekends may have realized how little they really cared for each other. Car poolers began to squabble, and when the gasoline shortfalls were over they went back with a vengeance to driving to work by themselves.

People cannot be compelled by some wholesale alteration of the immediate environment to care. They must have a reason to care and to be involved with others. In addition, caring must accompany a process of active sharing. There must be a religious (mythical and ritual) foundation for this sort of reciprocity. Sellers is victimized by pietist heritage which leaves the problem of community primarily an affiar of the inner "spirit." Furthermore, simply to reclaim existing institutions in the name of the "people" will not resolve the issue. The end of affluence will modify conventional living to the point where new kinds of institutions will have to be contrived. The federal welfare agencies, ill-conceived placebos for the disease of poverty in an affluent economy, are a case in point. It makes no sense to "turn over" the welfare system to the people when the people will be less and less able to finance it as it presently exists. The same could be said for the Pentagon and the entire federal bureaucracy. A post-affluent society will mean the scaling down of the labrynth of interlocking systems of business, government, and education spawned by abundance. The reason is plain. We would not be able much longer to afford such complexity and such profligacy of resources. The task of pruning the vast hierarchy of power and of cultivating new institutions will carry with it the development of appropriate structures of thought and behavior which make a more simple mode of existence viable. Caring for those whom we can no longer ignore because they share actively with us in acquiring our food or teaching our children will be made easier if we learn why we should care at all. Our purses may dictate co-operation with our equally deprived neighbors but there must be a deeper and more abiding rationale for co-operation over the long haul.

Such a rationale may be the charter of meaning for the community itself. The community exists because it tries to make apparent the "law of life," whether it be *t'ao*, *dharma*, *torah* or some yet unnamed principle. Relationships between co-workers, between older and younger generations, between man and woman must be codified experientially so as to allow for the growth and acceptance of binding norms, norms which are not merely capricious or factitious, but which somehow manifest natural commitments among human beings. To put it another way, a community must be erected on a more majestic ideal than the bare existence of the community itself. Traditions and the symbols of myth serve to articulate that ideal and thereby give it plausibility. Whatever new institutions come into being will reflect modified economic and environmental circumstances; they will represent the return to simplicity. But they will be justified through the knowledge that the humble and unambitious style of living is the optimal style. It is the optimal style of living because it is the most obvious and appropriate under conditions of scarcity. Religiously speaking, such a style is more in tune with the general nature of things. It does not overstep the domain of human possibilities; it is in keeping with the basic warrants of life as a whole. It is both more "natural" and authentically human at the same time. But what do we mean by "natural" and human?" The end of affluence will prompt us to re-examine our root assumptions about what these words imply.

Naturalism and Personalism

In his autobiographical and witty account of the triumphs and foibles of a California commune, Robert De Ropp talks about an earthy and homespun community of spirituality which he labels "the church of the earth."[11] The church of the earth has no inviolable creeds, top-heavy curia, or straight and narrow gate to salvation to which it has been entrusted the key. Its policy is like Luther's priesthood of all believers, except that the priests are identified not through personal faith but through the way in which they serve as chamberlains of the Eco-system. Such "priests" are indeed mutual teachers of each other, whose knowledge derives from an intuitive affinity with the world itself.

The tenor of D. Ropp's essay is that the "natural" manner of working and experiencing has little to do with eating organic foods, constructing A-frames from cut timber, or eschewing electricity to cower in the damp and darkness.[12] Romantic primitivism is a fool's paradise for modern technological man, just as the dream of boundless opulence and indolence has turned out to be a nightmare our ancestors could not have foreseen. To carry on in a fashion both natural and appropriate to our new situation will involve a re-organization of our personal and social lives that dispenses with the idle luxuries or frivolities of affluence while conserving those amenities that eliminate undue hardship and suffering. John Cooper, for example, has described in some detail what such a stripped-down style of getting about might be: trading the financial premiums of a job in a large corporate organization with all its pressure and ulcers for less renumeration, but with more family time and the chance to learn practical arts perhaps considered passé in an earlier generation. Shopping for bargains and low-budget items will have a certain merit taken in the past not as a mark of resourcefulness but of misfortune.[13] With proper societal checks against gross deprivation, the end of affluence will afford opportunity for many, if perhaps not all, to rediscover the dignity of making-do. The "something for nothing" attitude bred by affluence will hopefully be replaced with a disposition toward enjoying the most from the least, toward reckoning the simple accomplishments and rewards as not inane but joyous. This disposition can be acquired again within middle-class life. We do not have to opt for a rude economy of insecurity and discomfort. While romantic primitives have often attempted to turn the clock back to the stone-age and found themselves shockingly unprepared to do so, those adhering to the truly natural style will retain the best of twentieth century civilization and discard the worst. For instance, we can certainly envision a society which still values highly adequate medical care, literacy, and freedom from hunger or want, yet which does not give the same priority to owning frost-free refrigerators, going skiing every weekend, or having a bulging wardrobe. We can also imagine a society which esteems work as a vocation without extolling excessive drudgery or exploitation.

A problem can spring up, of course, if the drive for simplification leads to a preoccupation with austerity for its own sake. Austerity today is primarily a threat to people's psychic composure because they have lost the capacity to appropriate the symbolically mundane, to wrest meaning from the simple, and therefore they fear the boredom of having to do without the countless things which nature has supplied ready to hand. They regard austerity as a curse, because they are unable to gain fulfillment by any means except through constant accrual of the new -- new experiences as well as new possessions. Just as psychologists tell us that a certain amount of sensory deprivation can have the salutary effect of enhancing awareness and clear thinking, so social thinkers ought to instruct us that a reasonable degree of material deprivation can eventuate in a new appreciation of what it means to be human. Man needs challenge and struggle to achieve transcendence -- but not an overdose. More important, the prospect of austerity will appear less menacing only when the meaning of existence can be

reconceived for a whole culture as of something more uplifting
than Hawaiian vacations or ten dollar seats at a rock concert.
Austerity is not the same as either deliberate self-denial
(asceticism) or conspicuous consumption, both of which accent
selfishness and narcissism. Austerity is the condition of living
in some kind of ecological accord within the limits of personal
ambition, social solidarity, and environmental restraints. And
it is highly likely that out of this accord will come a deeper
consciousness of how the shards of the montage that is human
destiny fit together, how we can rightly distinguish, if at
all, between "natural" and "civilized" man.

The dilemma of what precisely constitutes the "natural" is
a prickly one, and any naturalistic religion and culture can be
properly described only when the issue is at last settled.
There is a tendency in civilization to draw a stark dividing
line between the natural and current society, as romantics
from Rousseau to Roszak have done. Thus the "natural" always
beckons as a bygone golden age recoverable only through some
apocalyptic collapse of the defiled present order. One may
surmise that the more *outré* and remote a person's conception
of the "natural," the greater the likelihood that that person
is quarantined within his own contemporary prejudices. Whoever
does not rightly understand the present is fated to distort the
image of the past. Whoever fails to discern the direction of
events in his own time will probably cling to false alternatives. Those who confuse the natural with the archaic and
the outlandish are probably infatuated with the archaic and
outlandish for its own sake. In this sense their sympathies
are quite "unnatural." Philip Rieff has phrased the irony
this way:

> The most efficient way to move closer to
> Nature cannot be to move backward, in some "life-
> style" indebted to modern imaginings of technolog-
> ically unprogressive societies; rather, Nature can

> only be achieved by moving forward, in transgressive breakthroughs that no historical "primitive" adopts in his own profoundly conservative way of life.[14]

Affluence and rapid social change have given the natural a wooden coinage because they have numbed all sensitivity to what is underlying and permanent, to what constitutes a consistently worthwhile basis for human endeavor. The "natural" look in dress during the last decade has really been a cloying artifice -- studied slovenliness or tawdriness whose only significance has been its sly mocking of the scrubbed and sterile fashions of the previous generation. Again, we have turned out, for the most part, to be rip-offs of dubious value. "Natural" sex becomes obsessive sex, without parallel even among bushmen or pygmies. The return to the undifferentiated unity of feeling and knowledge in some kind of primal ecstasy, as the new Dionysianism of the Esalen philosophy counsels, is no more natural than schizophrenia, R. D. Laing aside.

Natural man and natural religion do not invite an absolute break with civilization but a refinement of the recently emergent dynamics of civilization itself. The natural is not discovered in some myth of the primitive but in the hidden consequences of the life that is readily available. Man has never been, and can never be, as René Dubos has informed us, a naked wolfchild. Rather, the natural man has always been a steward of nature, forging and chiseling the raw materials of the natural world to make his surroundings pleasant and livable. Even the ancient Taoist sages experienced nature through their own well-tended gardens instead of through the untamed wilderness.[15]

The end of affluence should compel us to regain the sense of the natural, insofar as we will be forced to simplify our present endowments in a uniquely modern way. A sympathy for the natural, in turn, cannot be separated from a sense of the social, because man only becomes what he is truly meant to be in the company of his kindred. In this respect, too, the natural cannot be analyzed apart from the personal, providing that we understand "personality" not to imply autarchy and individualism but the specific realization of our human nature within appropriate biological and environmental boundaries. Human personality can be actualized in a fashion that is different from the Promethean quest of the West, the drive for individual detachment from nature and for power and control. Our personalities can be affirmed and developed within reasonable boundaries according to a unique kind of contemporary *Tao*, halfway between mystical immersion in nature and resisting the strictures of the natural order altogether. In a word, we must master the art of balancing and simplifying our lives so that we are not at the mercy of nature's whims (which we could not avoid if we eschewed technology in a lump), yet not presumptuous about our capabilities. We must find the least painful way of harmonizing with our surroundings. As Huston Smith has put it, "Simplicity and surrender can appear as highranking values only in a world one trusts and to which one feels at deepest level attuned."[16]

What concrete shape can be envisaged for such a realization of human nature? We shall have to give up trying to become, in Nietzsche's words, "suns for ourselves," fixed stars around which the needs of others revolve. Yet we shall also have to set aside any residual longings for a kind of life in which the claims of the self upon related selves could be resolved into some nebulous idea of the primitive collective. Marshall McLuhan and others have talked about a resurgent spirit of tribalism. Tribalism in the modern context has invariably served as the occasion only for mass egotism and the collective exercise of the will to power, as the Nazi episode suggests. If there is any surviving tradition in Western culture, it is bound up

with the myth of the reality and dignity of the person. The
question that the end of affluence prompts is whether the value
of the person alone can be affirmed apart from the value of
the person in community. With respect to religion, our Judaeo-
Christian heritage emphasizes the value of the person as discovered in dialogical relationship to the value of another
person. God addresses and calls man; man responds and swears
fidelity to God. The same is true of the relationship between
human beings. Martin Buber has written, copiously and convincingly, that the genuine life is the "life of dialogue."
The life of dialogue comprises an ongoing labor toward mutual
discovery whereby the meaning of existence is unravelled in
the intimate sharing of two or more lives, in an unremitting
appreciation of what each one of us has to tell about ourselves
and to learn about others through quiet conversations and
common involvements. The natural can best be defined, therefore,
in terms of the interpersonal, the simplest and most obvious
truths revealed through the words and deeds of our closest
associates.

Affluence has made the life of dialogue difficult to
master. It has left us absorbed in procuring rather than in
uncovering. It has severed the cords of trust and sincerity
in which the opportunities for deep sharing have been aborted.
There is something of a paradox in the fact that modern, technical civilization has welded whole peoples together at
impersonal levels of organization, in national bureaucracies,
in cities, in business and labor federations. Commerce and
communication in the form of superficial transactions have
been expanded and speeded up to a staggering magnitude. We can
forward messages instantaneously to our representatives in
Washington, get swift print-outs of information from far away
data banks. Yet we do not communicate in any profound or
effective manner. Politicians rarely listen to or understand

their constituents. The information we acquire through media is usually bland and without real content. While macro-organization has been perfected through systems management techniques, the connectedness of primary social groups has dissolved. The more tightknit and durable the community, the more feckless and irrelevant it seems. This is true especially of the family and the neighborhood. Yet it is only through these primary groups that true dialogue is possible, that our worth as persons can be recognized and affirmed, that the gleaming doubloon that is the ultimate can be exhumed from the sand of the commonplace.

The interpersonal makes manifest the natural. If the human self reflects the natural order, as the ancient Hermetic tradition held, it does so only partially. The bonding and intersubjective communication that goes on between selves in intimate encounters brings the partial reflections together. Just as the instinctually developing human infant must learn to use socially derived symbols and pattern its behavior after prescribed models before it can function in what we can call a "natural" manner, so the self-conscious adult must integrate his experiences with those of others in order to be in phase with the cosmos itself. Through communal solidarity man achieves a virtual entente with nature. The wild man of the woods is an aberrration of this relationship, not its paradigm. The "natural" personality only flourishes in a nurturing community. Baby monkeys, deprived of affection and sustained maternal care, for the most part grow up to behave in a fashion not befitting their species. Human beings removed from similar sources of love, recognition, and emotional reinforcement will turn out neurotic and barely at ease in what they perceive as a precarious environment. Similarly, the affluent society which has given us physical security and slaked our unappeased hunger for new sensations, though at the expense of atrophied community participation, has cut man off from his own roots. It has conditioned him primarily to respond to momentary arousals, to let him fall under the sway of temporary satisfactions while suppressing his natural disposition for compassion and fidelity.

The end of affluence will still modern man's lust for stimuli and the satisfaction of surface needs because such sources of gratification will be harder to come by. At the same time, the growing realization of the ways in which our personal lives are intermeshed with each other in the daily business of coping may well allow for mutual exploration of each other's inner mysteries and lessons. Again the thought of Buber is instructive. Buber, perhaps more than any other twentieth century philosopher or theologian, has assailed the modern idolatry of individualism, not so much on purely sociological grounds as mainly in light of the false kind of "knowledge" which it affords. The isolation of the bourgeois personality in his private social world has hastened the loss of both critical and confirming "feedback" from other selves. In consequence, experience itself has been counterfeited. The free spirits of modern culture have infused experience with breadth but not with depth. They have become locked into what Buber calls the "pretension of the false absolute." The authentic absolute emerges not from self-knowledge alone but also from a process of reciprocal engagement and penetration among finite selves. No knowledge of the infinite can be exhausted purely in self-awareness.

Indeed, to look for the springs of meaning in our own given consciousness leads to a fatal deception. The sources of life, the *Tao* of nature, is revealed in the sphere of the "interhuman," in a sharing community. Sharing is not only common possession and cooperation; it is also the give and take of open response and recognition. Members of a community must to more than care for each other; they must live in the tension of seeking to be a part of the inner lives of each other. As Buber say: "A society may be termed human in the measure to which its members confirm one another."[17] Such a society resolves the modern problem of identity insofar as it makes self-understanding into a correlate of what others can give to one, and one can give to others. One does not have to seek identity outside of one's community because one's community ministers to the deepmost search for recognition by the person. In the true community the shallow "semblances" of the person -- his role, his economic status, his biological form and structure, so important for the affluent society because they are what define his productive capacity melt away. In such a community "the semblance vanishes and the depths of personal life call to each other."[18] The obvious features of human communion are no longer obscured. When we dissolve semblances for the sake of a richer and more enlivened understanding of who each one of us is in relation to each other, then we go far beyond, for instance, artificial communality of feeling that characterizes encounter group testimonies. The point is not just to "bare all," but to listen carefully to each other's words so that the finite insights, anxieties, and longings of persons separately can be written together into an ever expanding biography of everyone together.

The principle of depth-encounter between persons, enshrined in the thought of Buber, can easily be misconstrued, however. Just as the ancient Hebrew warned that man cannot behold God face to face and live, so the modern who probes for total self-disclosure and confession will be overwhelmed. The modern temperament oscillates between total withdrawal and immersion, between the passion for privacy and public exposure, between complete repression and expression, between individualism and collectivism. Dialogue, though, is not a perpetual spring

house-cleaning of the soul. A community in which everyone was
constantly conversant with each other's thoughts and feelings
would be intolerable; it would trivialize relationships because
there could be very little surprise or wonder when one finally
came to "understand" another person. The mystery of the other
would become banal. It is similar, psychologically, to the
"bore" who does nothing but talk about himself, or to the jaded
traveler who has been inside the Taj Mahal twelve times. The
principle of depth-encounter does not necessarily imply that
people in community have things to do other than to lay themselves open from hour to hour. We really come to know another
person insofar as we are involved in his own mundane life
struggles, and vice versa.

Meaningful relationships between persons are predicted
on close mutual involvement in the tasks of everyday living
in tasks which embody a way that is most natural. Through
these tasks we become cognizant of the significance of the
life of the other; we do not have the luxury to be wrapped up
in ourselves alone. The rituals of community life provide a
sense of what is appropriate in dealing with others, and they
furnish maxims for affording the other the knowledge that
they are respected and recognized. If a man tells his wife
every minute that he loves her, she may begin to doubt his
sincerity, but he who decisively exhibits his love on special
occasions, such as on an anniversary or with the birth of a
child, will help to strengthen the bond of marriage. To put
it in another way: Christmas would no longer be Christmas if
it occured more than once a year.

Man and Woman: The Form of the Natural

The origin of a new revelation, therefore, must be in the
sphere of the interpersonal, but it must be an interpersonal
relationship that rests on tension and dichotomy, on a pull

between the secrets harbored by the other person and the desire
of the self to apprehend those secrets. It must constitute a
kind of breakthrough where the common experience is trans-
figured by some act or word of another person who contributes
to that experience. Traditions draw people in society together
through the power of shared meanings; it is, however, through
the ongoing interpretations of those meanings and the pooling
of experiences within a common frame of knowledge that such
meanings can become real and consequential. Revelation is the
process by which shared elemental meanings are made concrete,
or rounded out, by an interchange of different perspectives
and accounts. Revelation is the process by which the understanding of the other person is reconciled with *my* understanding,
a further concretion of meaning, takes place. The durability
of community, therefore, depends on the continuation of interpersonal dialogue. The preservation of the sense of "we"
comes with a mingling of the life-worlds of "I" and "you,"
which can only partially, but not completely, be assimilated
to the collective universe of experience. Myth becomes
revelation, in other words, to the extent that the familiar
stories and indications of the human condition are recast into
the very drama of *our* lives. Revelation is when a myth is
appropriated in a unique and personal way with relevance to
something outstanding that has transpired in one's own
experience. The core of meaning, the *kerygma* of the mythical
understanding, is given force through the presence of the other
person who makes the tradition come alive. Such was the case
with the personality of Jesus, who brought into vivid focus
by his own teachings and miracles what was implicit in the
legends of the Messiah but which awaited a charismatic figure
to bring it to fruition.

The myth of both the personhood and incarnation of God informs the body of primal religious meanings for the Western world. It is out of such a myth that a new revelatory pattern of meaning is bound to emerge. The decline in modern culture of the experience of a personal Deity, underlined in the "death of God" movement some years back, has been ascribed rather inconsiderately to secularization and to the fact that science has remapped the heavens. A personal God dwelling in the great beyond, according to this argument, is about as cogent today as the man in the moon. Such a God is, as Alfred North Whitehead remarked, like a "cosmic Cheshire cat" whose face and smile have gradually receded into the void of the space. Yet this argument sidesteps a more fundamental reason for the abandonment of the personal God postulate. Contemporary culture finds itself embarrassed with the "person" as a symbol of the divine because the sense of the interpersonal itself has slipped away. The person as a subject of respect and a vessel of mystery has disappeared, and in its place has risen the notion of people as things, as pale factors in the computation of social utility and economic performance. "Personal," when the word is retained at all, has come to connote the private and the insular. Thus, we search out God in our own solipsistic pipedreams or in the "collective unconscious." We do not reach out for God, as Buber has pointed out, in the reality of the "thou."[19] Our God becomes impersonal.

The tarnished sheen of the impersonal, objective world, as a result of the necessary disenchantment with materialist culture at the end of affluence, will bring into relief once more the sacred value of human beings, regarded not as instruments but as ends in themselves. Awareness of interdependence in the social arena will encourage this new religious revaluation of what is estimable life. Yet any rediscovery of personhood, as a value in its own right as well as an adequate image for talking about the transcendent, cannot be separated from a sensitivity to the forms in which personality becomes manifest. Heretofore, or at least within the legacy of philosophical and theological idealism, personality has been defined in terms of autonomy, in terms of the ontological supremacy of individual thought and consciousness. In keeping with the heritage of Immanuel Kant, personality has also been characterized within this tradition with reference to self-perfection and the cultivation of moral conscience and character. Psychoanalysis has, however, reminded us of the dependence of personality on biology. The women's movement, moreover, has driven home the relationship between personality and gender. While it has castigated customary stereotypes about "manly" and "womanly" nature, it has at the same time challenged us to pay heed to the feminine side of experience and personality. We have been shown that we cannot discuss the feminine personality on male terms. The concept of personality has within it an inherent stress or tension which Western thought has conveniently ignored in upholding partiarchal society and values. The strain is between the male and the female, between two unassimilable rival claims as to the texture of experience.

The personalism of Judaeo-Christian myth and symbol is finally straining under such duress. A feminist theologian, Penelope Washburn, has written that

> ...the fundamental error in using "person" language in religion, as in any institutional structure, is that it is unreal. I cannot become a "person." I am born a particular sex at a particular time in a particular place... My gender conditions my experience of myself and the world.[20]

Personality is a bivalent notion which cannot be compressed into a single category excluding differences of gender. Personality, in an ethical sense, entails not the independence of mind or self-consciousness but the interdependence of man and woman in

the most radical, existential way. The interdependence of
individuals in community is grounded, biologically and
metaphysically, in the interdependence of the sexes. If one
person lives in community, it is always in relation to other
persons. If one authentically exists as a person, it is
necessarily because one attains personhood, sexually and
experientially, through a relationship with a man or a woman.
The revelation that comes through the experience of personality, therefore, can no longer be confined to the ghostly
"God-man" Jesus. The revelation of the new age must flame
forth from an encounter and a commitment between male and
female. It is the profound otherness of sexuality out of
which the depths of life are opened wide and the critical
judgement on our private preoccupations and narcissism is
laid. If "Christ" is the "new Adam," the restoration of the
image of God, it is well to remember that the image consists
of male and female together. "So God created man in his own
image...male and female he created them." (Genesis 1:27)
The myth of the divine person, therefore, is intensified and
remolded through the revelation of our need for, and redemption
in, love and recognition by the other person, the other whose
reality is what we lack in order to be complete, and who lacks
what we have in order to become whole as well.

Male and female may well provide an indispensible clue
to a new religious sensibility in the years to come. A
recovery of the "natural" stance toward the world would certainly fit such a reintegration of the basic polarities of all
symbolism and experience, the male and female principles,
what Jung called the *animus* and *anima*. Stated theologically,
God is revealed as resolution of these essential limits of all
experience, which are sexual. As Karl Barth has stated: "Male
and female being is the prototype of all I and Thou, of all the
individuality in which man and woman differ from and yet belong
to each other."[21]

God can therefore be experienced fully only in relationship with a member of the opposite sex, in the depths of interpersonal life that must always remain the "two," but not the "one." The androgyne may be a sufficient metaphor for God as a conceptual totality, but not for the revelation or encounter itself which takes place through concrete sexuality. That revelation has not been possible before now because of Western humanity's domination of the natural order and corresponding denigration of the female. The subconscious mind of the West has typified in myth and custom woman as a passive subject of male hegemony in the same way that it has taken nature as a field for conquest and abuse. The colloquial expression about the "rape of nature" through runaway technology and affluence is more than metaphorically accurate. To incorporate the feminine into religious consciousness on a parity with the male is to redress the psychological wrongs which our culture has perpetrated. The sense of the truly "natural," of what is basic and simple, has been obscured by this age-old ban on the feminine in religion.

Ultimately, the sense of the natural is captured not in abandonment to the raw, procreative energy of sexuality (as in the worship of the ancient mother goddesses), but in the sanctification of male and female coupling in the institution of the family and in social ritual. The social equality of men and women will have to be a feature of the post-affluent society because of the eclipse of the male-inspired drive for power and acquisition. Both men and women will return to simpler tasks, from baking bread to raising children together. The simpler life will bring back closer economic collaboration between the sexes, since the division of labor as a means to specialized expertise and greater productivity will make less sense in a situation where the accumulation of material wealth is foreclosed by circumstances. "Mom and pop" stores or family farms may even come back into fashion. At all events, the joining of man and woman again for socio-economic reasons will foster a new awareness of sexual interdependence, and subsequently perhaps a fuller insight into the religious underpinnings of such a common life.

The natural "law" of human relationships as expressed in the male-female alliance will therefore become ritualized in a new society. A return to the same kind of "traditional" morals and manners in which the distinctions of gender are respected and rendered in appropriate fashion will go hand and hand with the new sensibility. We can learn again to love women as women, or men as men. We need not put women on a pedestal, or neutralize their sexuality by making them pseudomales. Nor need we feminize men. We can aim to develop meaningful habits and responses which, for example, symbolically consecrate woman's contribution to the life of society without cavalier definitions of "woman's place." The current myth of unisex and the vulgarization of sexual relationships have arisen out of the loss of sexual identity in an affluent era where interdependence is not recognized, where the cult of individualism has spelled sexual exploitation and conflict. The revelatory character of such a time-honored relationship -- the union of male and female -- may be difficult at the moment to grasp. The most simple and obvious truth may be the most formidable to digest or assent to. Mary Daly has written that the welling up of the feminine at the vortex of religious experience may be the most momentous event for millenia. Such an event is equivalent, Daly argues, to the "Second Coming."[22] The problem is, however, that we are prone to oversight in this matter. We await atop a mountain for angelic chariots to descend while the world is already being transformed out of sight down below.

NOTES TO CHAPTER 7

1. See Philip Toynbee, "Meditations on an Egg Tray," *New Statesman* (June 25, 1965), p. 999.

2. cf. Mircea Eliade, *Myth and Reality* (New York: Harper & Row, 1968).

3. Cited in Marcia Keegan, *Mother Earth, Father Sky* (New York: Grossman Publishers, 1974).

4. Herbert Fingarette, *Confucius: The Secular as Sacred* (New York: Harper & Ros, 1972), p. 36.

5. C. S. Lewis, *The Abolition of Man* (New York: The Macmillan Company, 1950), p. 16.

6. Lewis, p. 16

7. Lewis, p. 11.

8. James Sellers, *Warming Fires* (New York: The Seabury Press, 1975), p. 192.

9. Sellers, p. 177.

10. Sellers, p. 166.

11. Robert S. De Ropp, *Church of the Earth: The Ecology of a Creative Community* (New York: Dell Publishing Co., 1974), p. 44.

12. De Ropp, p. 298.

13. cf. John Cooper, *Finding a Simpler Life* (Philadelphia: Pilgrim Press, 1974).

14. Philip Rieff, *Fellow Teachers* (New York: Harper & Row, 1972), p. 152.

15. This view of ecology has been propounded in recent years by the French scientist, René Dubos.

16. Huston Smith, *Tao Now*, in Ian Barbour, *Earth Might be Fair* (Englewood Cliffs, NJ: Prentice-Hall, 1972), p. 80.

17. Martin Buber, *The Knowledge of Man*, Trans, Maurice Friedman and Ronald G. Smith (New York: Harper & Row, 1965), p. 67.

18. Penelope Washburn, "Authority or Idolatry? Feminine Theology and the Church," *The Christian Century* (October 29, 1975), p. 962.

19. Buber criticizes Jung for locating God in the depth of the unconscious rather than in the sphere of the Thou. Jung, Buber says, makes a *gnosis* out of monotheistic faith. See *Eclipse of God* (New York: Harper & Row, 1952), p. 79ff.

20. Washburn, p. 962.

21. Karl Barth, *Church Dogmatics: A Selection*, trans. G. W. Bromiley (New York: Harper & Row, 1962), p. 198.

22. cf. Mary Daly, *Beyond God the Father* (Boston: The Beacon Press, 1973).

A THEOLOGICAL POSTSCRIPT

> "True religion is a profound uneasiness about our highest values."
>
> -- Reinhold Niebuhr

The End of History

One word of caution ought to be advanced here. In the last chapter we discussed the recovery of a religious appreciation for the *everyday* as an appropriate option for living at the end of affluence. We also considered the rediscovery of the significance of personhood as nourished in marriage and in the communion between the sexes. No one should draw the conclusion, on the other hand, that we are simply proposing another "occasional" theology to mediate a number of ideological interests or favorite causes. We are not suggesting what might be misleadingly branded a "theology of the end of affluence." Our concern is an arrival of the end of affluence which may be construed as an historical event that somehow lends clarity to history itself. The Christian view of history, in particular, entails an intersection between linear history and what theologians have termed the *kairos*, a moment pregnant with historical portent. In traditional parlance, such moments represent the "judgment of God" in which the projects and proclivities of humankind are called into radical question. In the kairotic moment, the glib aspirations and sophisticated rationalizations of contemporary society are laid bare as sham and pretense. Much of what glistens is exposed as tawdry. The emperors have no

clothes. The assumed drift of history is presented in a new
light, and a deeper meaning to events hitherto obscured by
collective prejudice and self-deception is disclosed to those
willing to read the hieroglyphs in a new fashion. Prophecy,
no cheap futurology or entrail-reading, is a sudden grasping
of the internal structure of historical life along with its
far ranging implications. The end of affluence, therefore,
serves as the opportunity to take a different account of
the signals of human history which we are forever monitoring.

Modern culture, as many observers have tirelessly reiterated, has been obsessed with the "historical." By the same
token, modern man has proudly distinguished himself from his
archaic and feudal forebears by dint of his alleged appreciation
of historical dynamism and change, reputedly absent in "traditional" societies. Theologians of the postwar era have been
fond of accentuating the need for "openness" to the future
and to the process of social transformation. The once hallowed
virtue of "reformation" or renewal has become an *idée fixe*, so
that the prophetic challenge to the status quo in allegiance
to a transcendent set of values has been routinized and telescoped, lamentably, into the *cult of the new*. The quickening,
madcap pace of modern life has been subtly legitimated, at least
by liberal Protestantism, in terms of Hebraic categories, confusing wholesale change with "salvation history." Historical
change *in toto*, rather than its rare, revelatory moments,
masquerades as *kairos*. "Revolutionary" movements, whether they
be peasant, proletarian, or bourgeois in origin, are lumped
together uncritically as having supreme value. The peril in
this pervasive, latter-day "historicism" is that, while it
corrects those ideologies which give a bogus luster and a
counterfeit permanence to the existing forms of power and
privilege, it also succeeds in blinding us to the latent nihilism
in many revolutionary crusades that have been launched. Thus,

Reinhold Niebuhr's admonitions of almost thirty years back
still carry force:

> ...a philosophy which places a premium upon
> movement and speed will probably not inculcate the
> caution which the drive of a high-powered vehicle
> ought to possess. The uncritical confidence in
> historical development as a mode of redemption
> may have, likewise, contributed to our present
> disaster by heightening the historical dynamism
> of Western civilization to the point where it be-
> came a kind of demonic fury. We certainly cannot
> deny that the center of modern disorder lies within
> the very portion of the world which took a more
> affirmative attitude toward the drama of human
> history than the waking-sleeping cultures of the
> orient; and that this affirmative attitude became
> transmuted into an idolatrous confidence in histor-
> ical growth in the past two centuries of secularization.[1]

The end of affluence, we have insisted, may nonetheless prove the occasion for the end of the indiscriminate, historicist mentality that Niebuhr censured. Even now there are shadings of a fundamental resistance to the dogma of quantitative historical change. There are the political efforts to place limits on industrial expansion and energy consumption through the sometimes nebulous ecology movement, even though so many of the antigrowth advocates turn out, unfortunately, to be self-serving elitists more interested in esthetics or a particular *cause célèbre* than in real human community and the establishment of social justice.

But the end of affluence has greater consequences in the offing than the simple curtailment of extravagant life-styles. The end of affluence points to the "end" of history itself. By the "end" of history, of course, we do not mean an actual halt to man's collective venture in time. We are not seeking, like some Biblical fundamentalists, to construe New Testament eschatology in a literalist rather than a symbolic key. Our point is that the modern historicist attitude toward history (that is, the taking of raw historical movement as an unqualified good *per se*) has by and large lost sight of the Biblical realization that historical life must have both a purpose and a *closure*.

Mircea Eliade, in the concluding chapter of his book *The Myth of Eternal Return*, argues against the danger of historicism which in his estimation leaves man reeling from the "terror of history."[2] Eliade, however, opts for a rehabilitation of archaic myths and stories, especially those which embody belief in the *eternal recurrence of the same*, as a lifeline for man to pull himself out of the modern historicist morass. At the same time, Eliade tends to downplay the eschatological motifs found in the Old and New Testaments which work to keep the historical prospect from becoming a blank horizon while at the same time taking historical change seriously. In a word, by the "end of history" we mean some climactic point in historical time where the meaning of what has gone before can somehow become lucid in relation to what still is yet to come. History no longer need remain a roller coaster ride with its alternate thrills and terrors rushing around the riggings interminably. Instead, history can hold forth a *promise*. It can disclose the *kairos*. And the end of affluence can be regarded as an event in which a rich vein of significance is embedded.

The Second Coming

Hopefully, though, to designate the end of affluence as an instance of *kairos* is not to make the common theological misstep of imputing divine favor to the aspirations and ideologies of one's own age. Throughout the modern period, liberal Protestantism has recurrently fallen into the trap of making Christ into what H. R. Niebuhr dubs the "Christ of culture."

Certain finite cultural concerns are promoted as normative, kerygmatic, or definitive for the business of Christian theology. Recently this kind of theologizing has succumbed to the fallacy of what we label (adapting a bit from Alfred North Whitehead) the "fallacy of misplaced universality." A transient, particular moral or social objective is raised to the level of universality, precisely the fallacy Marx committed when he idealized the proletariat as the "universal" class whose victory over its capitalist overlords would lead to a classless utopia. So-called "liberation theology" has dallied with this fallacy most recently by attempting to assimilate the Gospel to the political intentions of certain oppressed groups. The elimination of oppression is not the governing issue here; nor is revolution in itself subject to criticism. The true question is whether certain self-interested, historical groups or movements should count as the guardians of man's historical destiny.

A "theology" proper to the end of affluence must not endeavor to give some kind of tenuous religious sanction to simple and austere lives, nor vaunt the new and necessary life-styles as somehow "holier" than those we have grown used to. The kairotic element in the emergent culture we have sketched so far resides not in the form but in the susbstance. The *kairos* may be seen as present not in any given historical state of affairs but in the *opportunity* such a state of affairs holds forth. The age itself is not the kingdom of God but contains within itself a glimpse of the kingdom not evident in the past. History is not revelation; it is the *medium* of revelation. The end of affluence, therefore, looms as the context for an unprecedented though not altogether unique understanding of the things of the "spirit."

The end of affluence, as we saw in the last chapter, activates the real possibility of a rediscovery of the meaning of persons -- persons in relation. The narcissistic pursuit of pleasure and ecstasy dwindles as a tenable life option, and in its place are posed the challenges of mutual relationships. The turning away from utilitarian and contractual relationships made possible only by a surplus of basic material satisfactions supplies the occasion for encounter with the other person in all his or her depth and mystery. Though material scarcity in past epochs did not yield such a realization of the mystery of personhood, chiefly because of the historical urge toward the easing of chronic economic deprivation, the return to relative scarcity in the years ahead will reverse the trend. Since the fulfillment of *minimal* physical wants has become an historical *fait accompli*, man can inaugurate the search for the spiritual ground of his own existence -- for the God within his midst. The search need not wander very far afield, for the treasure lies buried right in man's own field. The kingdom is near at hand.

The God who steers the bark of history, heretofore only a spectral and murky presence, now appears on the deck. The Christ "event" -- the "scandal" centering on the embodiment of the divine in human form -- is vindicated as the "end" of history. For now the revelation of God breaks upon us in the encounter between persons. The historical covenant in body and blood becomes a general bridge of fidelity among those who swear loyalty to each other. The connections of the divine with the human, attested and adumbrated in the man from Nazareth two thousand years ago, now emerges as a force that can transfigure all personal relations, if not the entirety of human institutions. The "mythical" Second Coming -- the yearned for "end of history" -- happens now as an unanticipated breakthrough. But the Second Coming is not the epiphany of the rider on the white horse -- the advent of the Son of Man in the earthquake and whirlwind. The Second Coming is not at all a singular "event" along the axis of historical time. It is the commencement of new possibilities for penetrating the ultimate. The ultimate is not described on high, nor in the hollow, reverberating caverns of lonely selfhood. The ultimate hints of itself in the most immediate and mundane of situations. It shows itself in acts of reciprocal love, trust, recognition, and commitment -- commitment to the depth and worth of all persons as they stand as potentially numinous presences to each other.

In previous eras man has compulsively sacrificed his kin and kith, including his wives and children, for grandiose historical undertakings. He has erected "pyramids of sacrifice" (to cite Peter Berger's metaphor), and christened them the "propagation of the kingdom." But at the end of history the kingdom needs no more to be propagated and there is no call for sacrifices. Hidden in what has many times over been put to slaughter, the kingdom again becomes the cornerstone which countless builders have rejected. The kingdom comes in the revelation of the other person within whom is reflected the gleam of the Wholly Other. God arises from the process of mutual penetration and disclosure. The "knowledge of God," therefore, is the knowledge which two finite selves in relation gain of each other's fathomless dimensions.

Beyond Idolatry

Yet the knowledge of God comes to be congenitally impaired by false constructions of the divine. The sin of idolatry is performed repeatedly, insofar as by "idolatry" we mean the adoration of the finite instead of the infinite, an enchantment with surfaces rather then depths. The most subtle yet widespread mode of idolatry in the modern world has been the reification of human personality. Paul Tillich has defined idolatry as "the elevation of preliminary concern to ultimacy."[3] When human personality is devalued to a proximate concern, as a "thing" or object whose worth is measured on a limited scale so that the "thou" becomes an "it" serving as an instrument to extraneous ends, then idolatry occurs. Certain abstract, or accidental, features of a personality, rather than the complex of infinite possibilities that each personality has, are taken as ultimate and as exhaustive of that personality's significance. The meaning of a person's life is delimited primarily in terms of his or her social status, occupational role, sex, intelligence, *credo*, and so on. Human personality as an intricate web of meaning and possibility is the receptacle of the infinite. Too often, however, the infinite is blocked from view because of finite allegiances and obsessions. A woman is "loved" only for her body; a generation is destroyed for the advancement of the "revolution."

Two principal forms of idolatry in this sense are epidemic throughout modern thought. The first form of idolatry is the definition of personality as some kind of generic membership. The second form is the converse of the first: the confusion of personality and individuality, or of "person" and "self."

The first mode of idolatry refers to the assimilation of personality to *persona*. The *persona* is the "mask," the outward and stereotypical public presentation of the conforming to certain general expectations about how people "as a rule" should feel, think, or act. Sociologically speaking, the *persona* can also be denoted as the *role* the individual performs in a system of associations and relations -- familial, political, economic, or the "function" he or she discharges for the maintenances of the larger institutions. *Persona* can also be understood with respect to class -- class identity as well as class mentality. Yet the *personality* is richer and genuinely more concrete than the functions and tasks of the self.

The ultimate aspect of the personality is always opaque to some extent, either because of the abstractions contrived by other selves to make the relationship "manageable," or because of the fundamental fact that the personality is forever a *potentiality* to be realized only when one's infinity and mystery gains recognition. Thus, the personality is not reducible to a class, a type, or a performance. As Martin Buber tells us, the "thou" discerned in the "other" resists limitation, classification, or abstraction. The "thou" is human personality in its infinite depth.

By the same token, those theologies or religious mind sets which look to the *persona* as the bearer of revelation run the risk of becoming idolatrous. Tillich touches on the same point when he remarks:

> Historical events, groups, or individuals as such are no mediums of revelation. It is the revelatory constellation into which they enter under special conditions that make them revelatory, not their historical significance or personal greatness.[4]

Liberation theology, for instance, tends to assign a unique, revelatory character to the revolutionary struggle and to confer some kind of hierophantic authority on the poor or oppressed *as a class*. The personality is subsumed under the conditions of class identity and its meaning is determined according to its role in the historical production. Those outside the class (who do not belong to the "elect") are *eo ipso* excluded from the scheme of historical revelation. But the incorporation of personality into class in this respect manages only to give an absolute significance to a finite historical cluster of circumstances. Potential for evil rises because a particular group can claim godlike preeminence on the pretext that it alone is carrying through the design of history. Here the contingent is raised to the necessary, the penultimate to the ultimate.

The second form of idolatry, though, is often perpetrated as a supposed challenge to the first. Existentialism and modern "humanistic" psychology, for example, have countered the claims of reductive behaviorism (a la B. F. Skinner, for instance) as applied to human conduct and history by asserting the premier value of the individual or the uniqueness of the "self." These schools of thought, nevertheless, mistake what is inidvidual as what is *personal*. The personal is made synonymous with the private. Man's solitary self-consciousness acquires the character of ultimacy. Carl Jung's theory that God is coextensive with the collective unconscious, apprehensible through exploration of the layers of one's psyche, is an important and influential illustration of the propensity to claim an apotheosis of the self, which in turn represents an idolatrous linkage of the finite with a false infinite. The individual self *in itself* can never encompass the divine. For the self is always captive to illusions of its making. One must look for the seat of divinity not in one's self but in the *relationship* between the self and other person. That has the potential for shattering one's own self-defensive illusions while at the same time, for mutual acceptance and discovery, it brings about a wholeness of personal existence that cannot come into being in solitude.

The revelatory potential of human personality which points beyond idolatry can thus be activated only in an *interpersonal* context. But the sphere of the interpersonal is not a given or immediate facet of life; it must be forged and shaped. The development of the interpersonal as the "space" wherein revelation takes place must be grasped in terms of its dynamic elements -- *judgment*, *confirmation*, and *commitment*.

In the Biblical narrative the meaning of history unfolds with reference to the transactions between God and his chosen people. God establishes his covenant with Israel and pledges his troth on the condition that his people also remain faithful to him, upholding the commandments and following in his path. The relationship between the transcendent God and his people is an interpersonal involvement. The covenant, entailing a reversible commitment to the wellbeing of each party, constitutes a set of mutual claims and representations on the part of each person toward the other. To transgress the covenant is to rupture the bond of trust, but it is also the sin of giving priority to the interests and illusions of the individual self. In disregarding the covenant man not only "turns his face" from God, he also denies the interpersonal context of revelation. He refuses the claims and shuts his eyes to the holy presence. He ascribes ultimate value to the concerns of his own finite and inconstant self. He spurns the deepest "knowledge of God," clinging to his own prerogatives and presumptions. He succumbs to his own narcissism insofar as he closes out the potentiality for personal insight and growth, and he balks at distinguishing between the open, infinite universe and the constricted world of his own fantasies and musings. In short, he is unwilling to lay himself open to judgment.

The idea of divine "judgment" is often confused with God's retribution. But "judgment" in the Biblical sense connotes something much more consequential than the wrath of the Deity, or divine chastisement. Divine "judgment" is bound up with revelation in the form of the entrance of God's Word into history. The Word discloses the truth which dissolves all delusions and idolatrous vanities. Judgment is, therefore, the smashing of the idols of conventional thought, the rigorous criticism of pernicious abstractions. The manifestation of God's might before Pharoah, for example, is suggestive of something else besides the punishment of the evil ones. "For I will pass through the land of Egypt that night, and I will smite all the first-born in the land of Egypt...and on all the gods of Egypt I will execute judgments: I am the LORD." (Exodus 12:12) The "gods" of Egypt, the false ultimates, are laid low. Judgment is the divulgence of new meanings which can only transpire when we are in the presence of the other personality who speaks the truth and assails our prejudices and excuses. In any "honest" relationship there is always the willingness to "judge" the other. That is not the same as condemnation, but the act of opening up a space for dialogue and mutual realization that is, nonetheless, thwarted when two people go about supporting each other's little lies and charades.

The saying of Jesus, "Judge not, that you be not judged" (Matthew 7:1) has often, and regrettably, been thought to imply that Christians should not take it upon themselves to criticize another, or even to confront another with one's honest perception of the other's dissemblance or falsehood. The setting of Jesus' words, however, must be discerned. It is a rebuking at the hypocritical and "judgmental" stance of Pharasaic religion which annuls the worth of the personality in stubborn defense of an abstract, impersonal good such as "righteousness." Subsequent utterances of Jesus in the same paragraph of Matthew clarifies this wellquoted assertion: "For with the judgment you pronounce you will be judged, and the measure you give will be the measure you receive. Why do you see the speck that is in your brother's eye, but do not notice the log that is in your own eye?" (Matthew 7:2,3) Every act of "judgment" in interpersonal exchange requires at the same time the dismantling of one's own ramparts and the disclosure of one's own vulnerable inner side.

The act of judgment, moreover, is in itself a movement toward *confirmation*. The other person is confirmed as an acceptable and lovable person, whose depth remains to be plumbed, *in spite of* his or her failings. In confirmation there is revealed a person that neither of the participants in dialogue had hitherto known. Judgment pronounces death to the false semblance the other person may erect about himself; it takes away the mask and lays bare the presence of a mystery. And the innermost nature of that mystery comes to light with the act of confirmation. The other person becomes a revelation to the "I" -- a true "thou." And the "I" itself is made clear to the subject of dialogue through the mediation of the other person. God appears in the space of the "between" as the holy presence sanctifying persons in relation. God comes when there is mutual discovery and recognition.

On the other hand, the possibilities for disclosure through judgment and confirmation depend on the fact of commitment. In the Biblical context the field of revelation is always the covenant. In the covenant God has opened himself to man, and man can no longer flee from or ignore God. A scientist cannot pursue his quest for knowledge of nature without a fundamental commitment to his object of inquiry. Likewise, a person cannot really "know" in an intimate and transformative way an other person with whom he is not radically and irremediably engaged. The mystery of the person cannot bear fruit until the mystery is observed, until the person is shorn of abstractions which make up its spurious status as a "thing" and given full play as a "Thou" as that which the person *can be* rather than that which the person appears to be. The true and astounding manifestations of the person is the manifestation (in a provisional sense) of the divine. But man too frequently looks for God in the empty heavens, or in the vacuity of his own ideological counters. Searching out God in the mirror of his own self, he envisages therein nothing more than his own wretched reflection glowering back at him. Man's quest for God as *God alone* inevitably winds up as idolatry.

The Living God

    Much of the interpersonal dynamic relevant to the theological brief we have given so far is described in a little book by the Swiss psychiatrist, Paul Tournier, entitled *The Meaning of Persons* and published in 1957. Like so many works throughout history, Tournier's book seems to have been far ahead of its time; and it is ironical, yet historically interesting, that *The Meaning of Persons* has not been taken seriously by theologians despite the author's profound theological conclusions. Tournier draws a distinction between "personages" and "persons" similar to our distinction between "persona" and "personality." The personage is all that is mechanical, routine, and typifiable in a human being; it is the facade, the function, the convenient function used for behavioral analysis and classification. The personage is what is cognized in our everyday brushes with each other and casual habits of relating. It is the *abstract other*, the part mistaken for the whole. The person, on the other hand, is that side of the human being in which lodges "the miracle of the presence of God." Although we range from hour to hour and day to day throughout an impersonal world constructed by our terse, survival mechanisms, there are instances (*revelatory* instances, in fact) when the personage explodes into the person with all power, depth, and mystery, which point the ultimate source of personality -- God.

    "The person is the original creation," Tournier writes.[5] The person is the *mysterium tremendum*, the staggering occasion on which God "calls" us, as he did Moses through the burning bush. But, unlike that of the burning bush, the person is not a singular and remote event shrouded forever in collective legend and memory. The person is a constant, potential presence within our very ken. The person is not some uncharted Hyperborea to which easy access is difficult but the portico to the

kingdom that lies on the very threshold of perception. The
person is the promise of history that is now an imminent
possibility within all of history. The person is the tabernacle, as Tournier puts it, of "the living God" who is yet
to become "transparent." That is why Tournier prizes among
all social institutions or conventional forms of relationships
the state of marriage and family. "There is only one supremely
privileged relationship in which we approach anywhere near
(transparency)," Tournier declares, "and that is marriage."[6]
The covenant of marriage, the commitment to family, in one
sense consists of simply one cultural expression of man's
historical life; in a more telling sense it bespeaks the very
source of meaning for human history. What in the past were
taken as mere metaphors for vague perceptions of the relationship between man and God now impinge upon us as concrete
forms of revelation. The simple becomes the sublime; the
ordinary opens up into the extraordinary. The living God
comes among us as a transcendent presence hallowing our meager
lives.

Such a God is the same living God who meets Abraham as a
friend and a companion, the same God who confronts the prophets, the same God who becomes immanent in humanity on the
Cross. But the immanence of God no longer has a single
historical reference point -- the event on Calvary two thousand
years ago. The meaning of the Second Coming resides in the
emergent possibility of encounter with God at the everyday
human level, in the clearing away of sacred space between
persons. The God of Abraham, Isaac, and Jacob has always been
a God who spoke to man, who was the Word who at last became
flesh. But we now live in the age of the "death of God,"
the death of a God for whom many can no longer hear the Word
or see the face. Though the Word has dwindled away in the
hubbub of history to the mere theological *idea* of the "God-man"

Jesus, the "death" of the Word points beyond itself to a rebirth; the withdrawal of the divine voice occasions a sudden, new proclamation. And the proclamation must be that the Word is audible in what is spoken between persons from the heart, in the dialogue held face to face. The Word become flesh in history culminates in the incarnation of the divine message in the still small voice of recognition and confirmation uttered from the depths of two lonely persons to one another. Such a realization may prove as much a scandal to some Christians as was the crucified Messiah to the Jews of the first century. The one who comes "has a name inscribed which no one knows but himself." (Revelation 19:12) The name is that of the other person whom we address in love, searching, openness, and humility -- the incognito Christ who hides the treasure of the kingdom, the infinite glory of the God in, yet present, at the end of history.

Summation

If "true religion is uneasiness about our highest social values," then what the end of affluence points toward is something more than an identification of Christianity with a new constellation of such values. To talk about the interpersonal as the ambience of revelation is not the same as to idolize certain social arrangements -- male/female role expectations, styles of life and forms of work, levels of income, types of political organizations. It is to map out the ground on which appropriate models of human relationality on both a small and large scale can be erected. Theology is not utopia-mongering, nor is it the mere defense and interpretation of traditional religious concepts. Theology is the symbolic formulation of an innermost historical message which passes the eye of journalists, historians, and social commentators. Theology is the discernment of *Heilsgeschichte*

("revelation history") which implies something more radical
and dramatic than the superficial application of Biblical or
"Christian" paradigms to the present. Theology is a search
for the secret of all human experience -- "religious" or
otherwise. Theology therefore recognizes the contingent but
only as an instance of the necessary. It takes the historical
conditions of life as conditions of that which nonetheless
transcends history. It engages in social criticism but not
for the sake of elevating a particular social position to
unconditional validity. Theology takes stock of the present
in order to read the future, not as future *per se*, but as
the opportunity for revelation still to come. There can be
no "theology of the end of affluence." There can only be a
theology for which the end of affluence is a kairotic sign
pointing to a yet unrealized complex of meaning. In this
book we have done an inventory of the signs, and we have
attempted to turn our faces in the direction the signs are
pointing. The way itself is still to be trodden.

NOTES TO THE THEOLOGICAL POSTSCRIPT

1. Reinhold Niebuhr, *Faith and History* (New York: Charles Scribner's Sons, 1949), p. 14.

2. cf. Mircea Eliade, *The Myth of the Eternal Return* (New York: Pantheon Books, 1954).

3. Paul Tillich, *Systematic Theology*, Vol. I, p. 13.

4. Tillich, p. 120.

5. Paul Tournier, *The Meaning of Persons* (New York: Harper & Row, 1957), p. 35.

6. Tournier, p. 135.

www.ingramcontent.com/pod-product-compliance
Lightning Source LLC
Chambersburg PA
CBHW070249230426
43664CB00014B/2461